Katmoran Publications
www.katmoranpublications.com
www.reincarnationbooks.com

ISBN: 978-1-939484-00-0

Copyright © 2012 Franki deMerle

All rights reserved, which includes the right to reproduce this book or portions thereof in any form whatsoever by the U.S. Copyright Law

Cover Katmoran Productions

CHILD OF THE UNIVERSE

by Franki deMerle

Also by the Author

Ripples on the Surface, first collection of poetry

Deception Past, a unique novel of reincarnation and past life identity theft told through Tarot Cards, as those involved learn to resolve betrayal with forgiveness.

Dragonfly Dreams, a romance novel about dreams that connect us, dreams that come true, and dreams that reveal the past. "There are places we can only reach in our dreams while our bodies sleep."

Five Flowers, a novel of five historical Tudor queens who reincarnate in Victorian London's Whitechapel district and again in the US in the 1960s.

Please visit the author's website at
www.reincarnationbooks.com

Please visit the author's page at
www.IndependentAuthorNetwork.com

Please visit KatMoran Publications
www.KatMoranPublications.com

Acknowledgements

All of Nature and humanity
Past and present
For as I've said before
Nothing I say is new
It's merely my own form

Each reader brings a contribution, and for this I thank you.

Special thanks to my sister Karen for all her support.

Special thanks to my dear friend Marta for all her help in everything.

Special thanks to Karen Hall, Lindy L, Gayle S, and Kathy L for their friendship.

Special thanks to William Potter, Terre Britton, EE Wilder, and The Independent Author Network.

Dedication

In memory of Beulah

Child of the Universe

Franki deMerle

103.

Un rayo viaja lejos de sol
Para calentar la hierba
Nunca ha conocido

*

158.

Arte de Dios
Realeza en todos
Infinito cactos alcanzan por el cielo
Zanjas y mesas a rayas en el desierto
Opaco y cerca el cañón grande
Natural y piedra preciosa árboles
Arte grandioso

*

Franki deMerle

290.

Clouds are swirling
Storm is brewing
Branches whirling
People stewing

I feel it coming
Barometer dropping
The weak come gunning
Fuses popping

No one wants to be wrong
But they don't agree on what's right
The friction's gone on too long
The tension's wound way too tight

Trees dancing in the darkness
Appear sinister to some
Living loose with no harness
Spirit free to have fun

Nature dancing freely
While constantly balancing
Seems to some unseemly
Frighteningly menacing

It's something inside
They're afraid to let loose
While living in darkness
Afraid of the truth

And those unafraid
Dancing along
Are part of their fear
Not allowed to belong

Child of the Universe

Nature is change
We cannot control
What Nature has made
Including one's soul

At odds with oneself
Is source of all grief
At odds with oneself
Artificial belief

Nature doesn't conform
It just is
What tomorrow becomes
Just is

*

291. Seven Wonders

Lasting logs
Of colored stone
Variegated bands
Each tells a story of the land

Joy and pain together
Opposites of the same
Yin and yang

Amazingly diverse
Runs true throughout
The Universe

Time the great deluder
Hopes and fears
Obscure the present
Under memory and pretense
Greatness an illusion
Humility a vision
Trust in the moment

The moment is the only truth
Right and wrong are ego abuse
Underneath all our fantasies
The moment stands alone
Holding all we cannot hold

Passion guides and overtakes
Each must know limitation
Are we empathetic enough?
Can we become compassion?
Empty spaces to fill with kindness

Many listen for the beat
Under the skin the heart's rhythm
Sings the time
Inside the soul of rhyme
Completed by melody of spirit

*

292.

Being nice is a tool
Used by the dysfunctional
The passive-aggressive
Often can't distinguish
Their own feelings
So they pretend and project
Realizing this is a big step for me
I used to be one-hundred percent feeling

Too trusting
Believing all on the surface
But sociopaths imitate
What is deep for the rest of us
As we each pretend sometime
To be what we are not
Being nice is a tool
Replacing empathy we forgot

*

293.

Beaded with incense
A flower spins
Its fragile petals
Into jewels that sparkle

In light that strengthens
Or snows that bite
Or rains that cleanse
Its sleep at night

Dressed in dewdrops
A flower cups
To catch, savor, drink
Of this life's dream

All light's spectrum
Concealed in its genes
Expressing the moment
As a passing thing

Passing onto its heirs
The variety it conceals
Gems mined from the soil
For light's spectrum to sparkle

Scented sweetly
With fragrant dreams
A flower leans
On its emerald stem

So delicate and thin
To soak deeply into
Its fragile cells
Fresh air of a breeze

Child of the Universe

Spirit unseen
Diversity freed
Through a flower

*

294.

Fate is carved like a coin
Heavier on one side than the other
Tossed at the time
Of every decision
It usually falls
Into a pattern

Spinning madly
Fate takes its course
Demanding heads or tails
From every person
The call determines
The gain or loss

And every step
Means another toss
While usually seen as gain or loss
It's all one
Changing each moment
Change is the moment

*

295.

As you read these lines
Please take no offense
They are merely results
Of my experience
On the outside of social cliques
Religion and politics
Dysfunctional family and school
Dysfunctional country too often cruel
To its homeless

We are born and die alone
No one gets special instructions
We're in this together alone
There must be a bigger picture
And then there's the fact I remember
Having lived before I was born
There are many of us
Some like me are stubborn
And hang on to the memory of it

The University of Virginia
Set out decades ago
To investigate and disprove
What many children know
Instead they discovered patterns
Continuity of personality traits
Facial structure similarities
Regardless of change of race
Or gender

Child of the Universe

And that was decades ago
This is not spiritualism
Its scientific investigation
It continues
The educated write their papers
I write my poetic lines
Some confirm through past life regression
Details of their prior lives

I have no college credentials
I write what's in my soul
Just as I learned to do
Two past lives ago
So take it for what it's worth to you
I share my thoughts herein
The method is from the past
The experiences are as I live

No offense is intended
Outspoken though I am
Trying to understand
All faults observed are mirrored in me
I share in all that's human

*

296.

How can one handle all of the pain
Without giving more of it away
You don't have to be part of the chain
The challenge is not to retaliate
Or blame yourself for being sensitive
Pain is a form of energy
Our bodies are made to feel pain
It tells us which way not to go
Except when it's overwhelming

If you can't run away
Fly away in your thoughts
Where you belong now is on Earth
Crying is no reason to be ashamed
Crying is just another way of bleeding
When your heart hurts
The tears will wash the wounds clean
And help you to see your way clearly
To look at the world differently

You're hurting because you want something
Someone isn't willing to give
You have to accept yourself as you are
And move on to continue to live
All other directions lead to pain
Give yourself everything you need
Because the people you hoped would won't
People don't love unconditionally
They advertise it but they don't

Child of the Universe

If you concern yourself with the people who hurt you
They'll hold you back and hurt you again
And you'll end up hurting yourself
The pain will get worse
Walk away now and love yourself first
It's not what they teach you in school
You'll never learn this in a church
You have to accept yourself as you are
A child of the Universe

We're each given a role when we're born
But nobody gives us a script
It can be fun making it up as you go
Instead of reading lines someone else wrote
I like to catch people off guard
And what happens next nobody knows
But it hurts when no one wants you to be part
Of their world
It hurts

We're taught that we have to fit in somehow
We're raised afraid of what others say
But our true goal is to be true to ourselves
The light inside is fighting to get out
Obscured by layers of dirt heaped on us
That we take in believing will help with the doubts
Our molecules once belonged to the stars
You don't need permission to be who you are
Breathe light in, breathe light out

Franki deMerle

Freedom is something you feel inside
When the moment is all that you need
Because you live by what you feel is right
You have to stay out of other people's greed
Or they'll bind you in shackles of what they believe
And you'll waste life playing their games
Forge your own path and find your own passion
The worst pain of all is the pain of rejection
Self-acceptance is air fit to breathe

I've been through all of this before
Another time, another place, but same soul
I didn't fit in and I couldn't pretend
To believe whatever I was told
What matters to some is being what's expected
What matters to me is being who I am
And the two don't mix
So I lived my own life
Quietly but free

And now they quote me
Here we go again
Trying to write what touches the depths
The feelings so deep, high and grand
Of the essence of being as deeply as I can
Who I am
And the celebration of all life around us
Others bulldoze, trample, and flounder
As I stumble into amazement—appreciation

Child of the Universe

Some don't let me take part in their lives
I'm not inviting them into mine
The planet is made of beauty
And an animal's honesty is fine
My cat when greeted gives me a huff
Always express how you feel
If someone steps on you yell loud enough
Cuddle for warmth when you need to heal
And say when you've been brushed off enough

If you want to play get the game started
If no one joins just play by yourself
Take plenty of naps
And watch out your windows
And rest when you're tired of yourself
These are the rules of my kitty cat
They work just as easily for me
We cuddle and snuggle and comfort each other
What more do two bodies need

Conversation can be manipulative
Acceptance is the language I speak
Committees and demands to change the world first
Holding a sign on a street corner and shouting at others
These things don't work
I've changed the world by being myself
Though few bothered with me til I was dead
Then others read me
Even pretended to know me
Made some of it up out of their heads

Franki deMerle

But I tried again
Got more active
Even tried to fight in a war
War is deadly
Blood is shed
Baked in an oven until I was dead
But they had to change that up as well
The truth too unpleasant to tell

So here I am again
I tried to play games again
Now the pain is a pain syndrome
Electricity leaps through space to excite
A painful neuroreceiver
Replace it with a receptor of peace
Replace it with none at all
But a writer must write and a poet must feel
So I'm playing electric ball

But space is the key to winning
Let lightning pass me by
While I breathe in my space of becoming
A serenity artist who writes
Pain is a wake up call
An alarm, an announcement device
To look in the mirror at who's really there
A child of the written verse

Child of the Universe

The body ages, sags, and fails
Layers slough off like discarding a veil
Of past life abuse, rejection, rebuke
And suddenly there's nothing left to prove
It's all written down
Edited and altered
But it's survived as a written record
Of whom I have been—
Who I am

Anyone tells you their death didn't matter
They lie
If they try to live back in their former life
They weren't there or they didn't learn the first time
You don't want to relive the pain
Remembering keeps the soul moving on
To try to leave the pain behind
The goal is to either out run the pain
Or stand perfectly still in time

I've been there and tried them all
The only thing works for me
Is reaching inside to who I really am
And setting the starlight free
I write this now perceiving a need
For what others might do when realizing
The awful pain of awakening
I've three lifetimes of experience explaining
Set your inner spirit free

Franki deMerle

The pettiness keeps on revolving
But is so quickly forgotten
Fear spawns hatred so don't be afraid
You are all you have
Don't fear yourself
Fear is what leads to shame
Another day spent is not wasted
If it helps you find peace with yourself
If it helps you break free of your chains

You may have guessed by now
I'm writing this poem to myself
In case when I'm born I forget to remember
To get on about being myself
Some might say it's narcissistic
I say they're thinking in fear
I'm just being realistic
I know whence I come
And I'm here

Here to say it one more time
Here to word it a different way
All I am is rhythm and rhyme
All I am is ebb and wave
All I am is spark and ash
That burn with pleasure and pain
I am no longer afraid of my worst
No longer deluded by promise of gain
I am but one in the verse

*

297.

Old growth shelters the new
Raising limbs to the sky
Evergreens and ocean blues
Growing toward the light
On the sea breeze a healing breath
Needs only to be inspired

*

298.

I grew a purple flower
It mated with a white
And there were little blossoms
So beautifully striped

I smelled the purple flower
It smelled just like the white
But to the little blossoms
They were the same in smell and sight

*

299.

If the Chinese hadn't ousted him
Would the Dalai Lama have spoken to us
Or kept his knowledge in Tibet

For those the Chinese killed are back
You cannot murder spirit
Some will remember

Some will tell
And we shall all relive it
It never ends

We never learn
You cannot covet wisdom
Like raindrops falling

On the earth
It will insist we share it
And we'd best learn to hear it

*

Child of the Universe

300.

A leaf inspires
A leaf expires
It expresses the all
Of the limb it squires

Converts the light
Into its feed
Tiny stomata
Engorge the tree

Where minerals meet
After upward journey
Celestial excesses
Within the leaf

The tree discards it
It falls so freely
Upon the breeze
Into gravity

And such a blessing
That here may linger
A resting leaf
Upon my finger

*

Franki deMerle

301.

Valley of lakes and Christmas trees
Air so clean it's sweet
Next to Mount Saint Helens
Columbia River bends
Over the river the waterfalls
Underneath Mount Hood
Vast flocks of geese and seagulls call
Echoing over the woods
Restless migrants all

West of the Cascade jewels
Along the Pacific coast
Sea lions, salmon and whales
Have shared the deep with the boats
In spring and summer flowers
Nurture the tender berries
Growing all around
The rose, lilac and lavender fairies
Offer flavors that astound
Nature's abundant harmonies

*

302.

Salty oceans swallow the snow
Muddy rivers carry it slowly
To oceans

A snowflake may seem drowned or lost
But look again at fresh formed frost
A bit of snow has been reborn

*

303.

Your Goddess watches over you
The Goddess of Compassion
And of Sacrifice as well

In all that you've been going through
In this world's confusion
The sacrificial realm

She knows the deeper truth
What you think you have forgotten
Sings in the ringing bell

*

304.

Pourquoi dois-je faire des vers?
Qu'est-ce que je devrais être?
Laquelle est plus importante—
Etre une poète ou être une amie?

Ce sont l'une et l'autre partie de ma vie
Si j'étais une poète
Je serais toujours seule
Je ne peux que faire des vers

Quand je suis seule
Les autres hommes revivraient ma vie
Mais je l'écrirais seulement—mais si
Je cherche à être une bonne amie

Je ne serai jamais seule
Je suis une poète mais
Je ne voudrais pas être seule
Ainsi fais-je des vers pour mes amis

*

305.

Illumination of reflections
In the light we see
But only through interpretation
Delusions misperceive

How easily we fool ourselves
Convinced by misbelief
Limitations hide the will
Disguising our true strength

Child of the Universe

Thought creates activity
And leads us to discovery
Encountering society
That brings no kind relief

A culture built of outer shell
Not knowing what's inside
Requires reflection of oneself
To bring the truth to light

Nature verses society
The natural versus technology
The men must always fight
Or compete to find what's right

Diversity is Nature's way
Tolerance brings harmony
The women must cooperate
For survival of their babies

Is technology the master or the slave?
What price is put on life
When people are told it must be done?
Don't they have the right to decide?
The paradox of power
Is what cannot be controlled
Leaders will only be followed
If chosen by the fold

Is the glass half full or empty?
Regardless there's room for change
Traditions evolve or are broken
Nothing stays the same

Franki deMerle

When power becomes aggressive
The passive march in spite
Of vain attempts to control
What they know in their hearts is right

We choose our path to illness
We choose our peace to health
We only choose each other
With roles we play ourselves

The heart speaks through its passion
It follows to the end
It must express compassion
Or plant new seeds to tend

Truth always wins
It just simply is
To deny or accept
And thus determined

The truth simply is
That life moves on
The river keeps flowing
And dark turns to dawn

Balance is not stasis
It is a practice of process
Troublesome but relentless

It's who we are
It's what we do
It's nothing new

Child of the Universe

When surrounded by darkness
Find the light within
Follow the wisdom of the heart
When you stumble, begin again

You can't escape who you've become
So simply take a stand
Defend yourself for all you're worth
And bloom where you've been planted

The world is whole just as it is
And it is ever changing
We ride along for good or bad
The wheel is always turning

The choice of how we ride is ours
The centered keep their balance
And all the Universe will share
With beauty, love, and kindness

Courage for the challenge
Is not found in anger
But in gentleness

Changing times bring changing ways
And some catch on too late
Opposites compete for space
But only forgiveness can overcome hate
Find your passion and pursue it
Live your feelings and transmute them
Pain feels like a death
A cicada climbs out of its skin

Franki deMerle

Mind and body
Death and life
Duality inherent
In dual sight

Even the boundaries
Sands and tides
Are blurred together
And lost in time

Shadows only fall
When light encounters obstacles
Time gives a security
That something new will follow

Habit turns obsession
Trying to control
A feeling, a sensation
A need for something more

Free will blindly follows
Giving up control
To madness and delusion
Lost in shadows' hold

Devastation shudders
Walls have crumbled all around
After the dust settles
A ray of truth is found

Child of the Universe

Overwhelming darkness
Obliterates the stars
When questioning arises
Things are seen for what they are

The Dreamtime frees our hearts to soar
To fly among the stars
In waking when we've closed the door
Trust visits in the dark

Sometimes the world offers no way
We have to close our eyes
To follow the road of our dream
And trust in changing Time

Dreams misunderstood are madness
Dreams ignored reflect around us
We create our limitations
And act surprised when they surround us

Pretending to not be oneself
Distorts the mirror image
Worse is hating one's own self
Denying the inner message

Now has come full circle
Now is all we have
We are but a moment
Culmination of the past

Frightening to feel betrayed
But we are no different
Hating someone's such a waste
When we all seek forgiveness

Franki deMerle

Guilt haunts those with conscience
Fear of being wrong
Everyone craves innocence
The river rolls along

Until it empties into the ocean
No longer forced to bend
By boundaries and limitations
Life begins again

Break it down to atoms
Down to quantum bits
All of it's connected
Every molecule fits

All is interconnected
In a gravitational dance
None singled out or selected
An equal game of chance

All seen in varying perspective
We choose which view to take
A species so selective
The choice is ours to make

Forgiveness frees the fetters
Dreams display the dawn
Compassion brings connections
Time travels on as one

*

306.

Coast lined with sea lions
And zebras in the fields
Lying in wait the Santa Ana winds
Intend to make all level
Fires consume the rich and the poor
Or mud slides them into the sea
Riding the collision of continental plates
Nurturing the vines and the grapes
In the balancing dance of the ages
As Lassen waits to threaten Yosemite

*

307.

Animals have no conditions
They love with all their hearts
They teach us and befriend us
All too soon they must depart

The pain of separation
Is as great as the love
So don't be ashamed to express it
Time never is enough

*

308.

For every day there is a season
To every life there is an end
For every crime there is a reason
Though we may not comprehend

*

309.

Much time lived here
And much revealed
Seneca memories interfered
Societal pressures to be healed
Alone in the night insights were found
Comfort of family all around
Hearing Nature's call
Ultimate wisdom to find sound
Subtly hidden in gentleness
Everywhere else the country's in madness
Try to remember
Try to forget
Simply be in the present

*

310.

It's OK to admit you're sad
I suffer from depression
From all the world's insane conquests
And madness of acquisition

The emptiness where joy should thrive
Appreciation for being alive
Lost on those who risk it all
For what they think is greatness

Power to control others
Power to decide for them
Is hate concealed by domination
Is lack of reason to live

Fear and pride of protection
Is another excuse to control
And enforce limits by deception
To camouflage the void in the soul

Just say no to scare tactics
Fail to acknowledge the bullies
Just let go of insanity
And contemplate the beauty

*

311.

One verse, one existence
The essence of intelligence
The moment of awareness
Is intention
Communication is the desire
To share information

Those that choose to counter
By labeling something secret
Try to hide like cowards
Build walls to block themselves
From remembering what is kept
Within their cells

Knowledge already exists
We already share access
To the Universal unconscious
Our purpose already discovered
To desire to deliver
To one another

*

312. for Denise D

Of all the beings in the world
I shared a space with you
Of the many people you have helped
The children at your school
And teachers and administrators
I'm proud to be one too

Child of the Universe

I grew up in a violent time
I dared to cross a racial line
So I am one you'll never find
In a classroom
But I also know the brightest minds
Must run to keep up with you

Many value position and rank
Many value degrees
I value degrees of progress and strength
Of kindly gentleness
I value your determination
To give everyone your best

No one can control others
This the wise woman knows
One befriends through kindness
Those who are willing to love
The rest are thrashing injured birds
When healed will fly like doves

There you are in the very middle
Of the thrashing chaotic mess
Calming those you are able
Helping broken wings to set
Teaching stressed out teachers
With your intelligence

Someday wisdom will arise
In a country that lost its way
And we will actually value the wise
Instead of entertainment and sensation
But until that time
Please teach them with your patience

*

313.

I cannot comprehend the chase
Desperate Christian greed in haste
Attacking simplicity for land
Hunting down families—so much waste
Oh for Chief Joseph to return again

*

Child of the Universe

314.

We have a purpose
We find it on different levels
We see a vision and pursue it

And somewhere in doing
We break through it
And understand why we're here

We face each other every day
And still we can't communicate
There is no wrong except for hate

There's no need to condemn
We reach too far and miss the point
There's nothing to defend

It isn't ours
It isn't theirs
There is no us and them

*

315.

It's real
After all these years
The memories
Are real

Liberté was the word that carried me
From one life to the next
An unfailing, unchanging memory
Of one last escaping breath

They slammed the oven door on me
They could not incinerate memory
Burn the body, burn the books
But here I am writing poetry

They say there's no physical evidence
Those who don't want to believe
They're afraid that in the cosmic dance
It's themselves they'll have to meet

It's true
You cannot escape what you think
So true
Death is merely a blink

Of eyes that change color
But still look the same
Evidence, you say?
The pattern is the game

Synchronicity
Simple coincidence
No other way to explain
What actually exists

Child of the Universe

Birth marks and defects
Talents innate—not learned
Knowing how to rhyme
Knowing I was burned

The wrong person was accused
An award that wasn't earned
The stories we all tell
To teach the lessons learned

An Alabama girl
Writing ragas on sitar
Living in an inner world
Lit by a fallen star

Knowing that the South was dead
The war for slavery lost
While all around the bigots said
Kindness was too high a cost

Watching with a bitter taste
As memory of the Holocaust
Became the reason for more hate
And slaughter

It's real
People will be cruel
Judge the mirror
Forget the duel

Different gender or different race
You come back with basically the same face
It's simple really
We're all one race

Franki deMerle

It's here
Heaven and hell
Purgatory too
Nowhere else

Why so many people now?
The intervals have changed
We used to wait for years to return
But so many babies made

Allow us opportunity
Instead of decades or centuries
We are reborn more quickly
And with fresh memories

And as such there is history
Written of our past
Waiting for discovery
Of whom we were last

It's not a dream
Life's just a dream
We take it all so seriously
Just flow downstream

A dam will only last so long
A flood of memory will break through
Man-made religions are not strong
Enough to change the truth

We live in patterns
Our neural net
Is just an imprint
We can reset

It's real
It's true
I remember
I can choose

*

316.

Nothingness is something powerful
Even man cannot destroy
Vacant mirage of arid mountains
Allow the sky its joy
Dust fills the endless palette
At every sunset

*

317.

Depression is the poet's curse
Sensitivity hurts
Awareness of feeling not forgotten
Burns

But the truly mentally ill
Are those ignoring reality
Trying to force their will
On the rest of humanity

We have an inner rhythm
We can follow naturally
A word can strike a chord inside
If we are listening

The insane make much noise
It isn't harmony
If we're quiet long enough
And listen
We can hear truth sing

*

318.

The elemental play of change
Often perceived as pain
Has spaces in between
Fleeting glimpses point the way

Like reading between the lines
Images from within abound
Await the inner realization
Of the beauty found

Child of the Universe

Between the earth and fire
Lies the spark of light
Extinguishing desire
And giving wings to flight

Between the air and fire
The changing of the seasons
Winter's cozy hearth
And summer's playful freedom

Between the air and water
The rainbow will appear
Eternal hope it fosters
Random beauty in the clear

Between the earth and water
Springs the will of life
Diversity of Nature
Flowers bear fruit til ripe

Between the earth and air
The secrets on the breeze
Whisper in the ear
Of what we do not see

Between the fire and water
We see the dead reborn
What was a painful parting
Is joyful when reformed

*

319.

Vagrant leaves swirl around
Exquisite orange and gold
Red trees stand tall and proud
Mountains of color explode
Over the eyes and into my dreams
Nights filled with warm colors and chilled
To delight my wildest imaginings

*

Child of the Universe

320.

Few care about poetry anymore
It requires a presence of spirit
Now occupied by constant motion
And noise

Bombardment of the senses so
There is no presence of the moment
No depth beyond the spoon-fed
Consumerism instead of culture
Once a soul now dead

No one listens anymore
Tone deaf by obscene rap
And nasal wailing where once was song
Global commerce sounded Taps
When CEOs determined products
That stole the joy of a laugh

*

321.

There are milestones we pass unaware
Our unconscious knows they are there
The age which we died before
More intense than any anniversary
Of some other loved one's death
If we don't realize when it is
It seems like such a bizarre event
And illness or injury suddenly steps in
To stop us in our tracks
So we can contemplate where we've been
And take note of the facts
Life is not just linear
All our past is woven through
And we knit past and present together
To wrap around our future
The present moment simply is
Made up of woven strands
From all of time enshrouding us
As we pretend to live
As if all that we see here now
Is all there is to being
It's time to open the inner eye
And find what we've not been seeing

*

322.

Western white isolation
Yields extremist thought
Ordinary people thinking
Mediocrity is superior to love
Indigents had a different perspective
Not wanting to be bought
Guns, arrogance and greed cannot

*

323.

Solitary thoughts
Direct interaction
What are we accomplishing here?

We devise security
Systems to protect us
From our internal fear

The social fool has wisdom
He tarries but to laugh
At all the silliness we conjure
To bury our own past

We change up sides
We play again
We war as if to win

The fool knows
All death's in vain
As we are here again

*

324. for Christy

You have the key to peace
You know where beauty is
Not at the destination
But during the journey

Thank you for showing me how
To walk purposefully into the center
And be the essence of who I am
Relaxed, enthusiastic, and together

The slower one is in getting there
The more one sees along the way
The subtleties rich in color
Feeling through the feet what is ancient

Connected in the end to oneself
Connected to the center of One
Connected to past, present and future
It is done and it is begun

*

325.

Nice people wanting to lend a hand
Except manure everywhere smells bad
But maybe they get used to it
Riches of grains on the plains
Ain't translated into wealth
So virtual the culture has become
Kernels of health can't reach far enough
All the poor can't buy the farm

*

Child of the Universe

326.

The sunlight wrestles with the clouds
To sneak a peak below
At all the ways the people play
With whatever each one knows

Each beam of light a moment in time
Refracting into particle beings
Alone and together a whole
They destroy and then they build again
Inventing sense of purpose
When all just want to be comfortable and safe
Within a constant state of change

Too much sun or clouds or rain
Or not enough can bring such pain
The sunlight wrestles with the clouds
No effort, no worries, no struggle
Just Nature's spontaneity

It's not about ease or difficulty
It's what's felt and seen while looking out
It's the interplay of everything
For the joy and appreciation
Of the beauty in the ever changing
Panorama of our whereabouts

Decay and death and violence
Are elements of all change
The blend of paints upon the palette
All we see are gallery splatters

Franki deMerle

We are merely studio visitors
But for all our self importance
No one has a starring role
Some claim to know the director
Or predict how the story unfolds

But the glamour is too far beyond us
The picture too big to behold
By tiny creatures worried and scared
Until the realization dawns
That comfort must be shared

Clouds come and go and drift apart
Their tears the life of rain forests
And shadows cast below
For even in the total darkness
Acts of kindness glow

We build up clouds of fear and doubt
Shaming others for falling ill
Or not meeting expectations
In our nest of world imperfections
And all too late the shame descends
For kindness left abandoned

Yet even here we hold out hope
For yet one more distinction
Between those done of illness or pain
Or done of pure intention

Child of the Universe

Eventually the cycle shifts
A greenhouse forms or clouds dispense
An unguided fleet of ships adrift
Impervious to those separated
By choice, accident or stealth
The wisest are those driven out
Exiled from the tribal wealth

It's not a matter of survival
It's not about us at all
The bigger picture lies far beyond
Whether we stand or fall

The sunlight passes over the clouds
It travels to wherever it goes
It shares its warmth or searing heat
For its uncaring consequence
We let it reach our skin and brains
And in that instant if aware
Become one and the same

And that is unconditional art
To share its essence and become part
Of what is beyond ourselves

*

Franki deMerle

327.

My nightmares are returning to the past
I don't want to go back
I prefer to move forward
I'm always ready to move on

I don't want to go back
To pain I've lived before
If there is pain on the road ahead
At least it's something new and fresh

Times gone by belong that way
Love lost is gone—not worth finding
Surprise is the joie de vivre
Patterns wear out—become tiring

No desire to revisit childhood
Wasn't happy then anyway
No desire to return to a past life
It's already dead and decayed

Let me move on and keep going
Freedom isn't found in the past
Least not if you're a woman
I'm grateful the times change fast

Still it's best to know who you are
Identity points the way to one's goal
Follow the patterns that led you here
And see the big picture unfold

*

328. for Carol

You have a laugh hearty and deep
Revealing a heart of true joy
Not shallow, but rich with meaning
You have a voice that speaks
As if Mother Nature herself were speaking

*

329.

The creator of this Universe
Left no possibility out
Diversity is the name of this work

The blind turn to conformity
The darkness of the world
A blanket of false security

The helpless seek control of others
Charming talk and shrewd arguments
Seek positions of power

The traumatized may listen to them
Fanning the flames of rage
Adults who are emotional children

Tolerance builds a gentler place
Where kindness finds a peaceful way
Allowing acceptance to finally feel safe

Matter can only change
And energy cannot be destroyed
Transmutation of pain

Franki deMerle

The feeling of looking up at the stars
Overwhelming, humbling at first
Then you realize that you are part

Of all of this
Of all that exists
All part of creation's essence

We are children of the Universe
And children of the Earth
Life should be celebration of mirth

Anger is a separatist thing
Tolerance lets you feel the flow
Of infinite energy

Wake up!
We can choose
We are free

*

330.

Happiness is natural
Aloha rainbow state
Watery emeralds of swaying palms
As long as the balance of lava and sea
Is maintained
Its balance is harmony

*

331.

Mercurial messenger hones her skill
But cannot communicate
Unless the reader can be still
And contemplate

Generations struggling still
With hate over education
Dare to claim that they are great
Without communication

And so the messenger begs again
To see, to hear, to listen
Intelligence is all around
And so much more than human

I cannot stop—I am compelled
To speak out yet again
The Earth is full of wonder
Where there is life is wisdom

*

332. for Rhonda

You are my friend
You are a happy face
Your very presence
Released my depression into space
Namaste

*

333.

Traumatized people fear change
It can bring stress and pain
Into lives barely making it
Day to day

Traumatized people are emotionally immature
They don't function like adults
They aren't quite rational
They don't know how to ask for help

Traumatized people pass it on
To their children, families and friends
They scare their neighbors and cause commotion
When adversity needs to end

Traumatized people are impatient
But masters of knee jerk reactions
As long as no thought enters in
They repeat mistakes again and again

Traumatized people don't see there is so much more
They hide behind a veil
Of conspiracy theories and suspicion
Because they are not well

Traumatized people come home from wars
To which they should never have been sent
Because all society suffers the cost
Of their torment

Traumatized people had parents disturbed
Who could not nurture their children
It's all about them
Even when it isn't

Child of the Universe

Traumatized people grow up cruelly
With traumatized parents and sadistic clergy
Who teach them fear and rage
And expect conformity

Traumatized people are dangerous
To themselves and others they love
But fear and pride and ignorance
Keep them from rising above

Traumatized people don't know they're sick
They think it's the rest of the world
Easily shattered by haunting memories
Emotional ghosts that hurt

Traumatized people are afraid
They don't know how to forgive
And let go of their habit of hate
So they can learn to give

Traumatized people have exaggerated laughs
And tense up when trying to have fun
It's hard to relax when you're in so much pain
And you're always afraid of what you might have done

Traumatized people don't know it's ok
We're all human and all make mistakes
It's ok to let go and have a good time
Enjoying life is never a sin

There is no hell except the one you're in
Forgive and let go of the judgments
Live again

*

334.

Nestled in wet mountains
Of four seasons
Rites of passage
Tobacco plants
Harvested for death

Condensation every breath
And no one seems aware
Rather folk art proliferates
Over common care
Legacy of separation
Institution of pride
Nestles—hidden in the hills
Almost lost in time

*

335.

Sometimes truth isn't pretty
It hides an inner beauty
But when you judge
You do not see it

*

336. for Jackie

Your crown is the white of angel hair
Inside you have the strength of a bear
The balance is in just being here

*

337.

Illness is a metaphor
A spiritual expression
A concrete presentation
Of what is left undone

Diagnosis is symbolic
Of the needed recognition
To remedy the rendition
Of the tormented soul

It speaks unconsciously
It speaks metaphorically
The point is it speaks clearly
On multi levels spontaneously

But we of tunnel vision
Focus solely on the symptoms
That plague our physical existence
And mirror mind and emotions

The being is a whole
When there is sickness in the soul
In so many ways it shows
Until the mirror knows

Our dreams are not per chance
They always tell us first
When we don't heed their stance
The body turns for the worst

But never randomly
Only logically
The symptoms speak
Of what we need

Franki deMerle

There is no shame in illness
This must not be misconstrued
It simply is a message
For the one who needs its use

It never is a judgment
Though sometimes a cry for help
More accumulated patterns
Ready to free themselves

Illness is so personal
The healthy cannot understand
Its private communication
Those not privy may lend a helping hand

Or just shut up about
What they cannot understand
Or they will have their turn
At pain they have condemned

Only the person suffering
Has privilege of the dreams
That offer insight and understanding
Of most unpleasant things

Dreams are communication
Personal and internal messages
And those that don't receive them
Are not getting healing rest

Child of the Universe

Those that just ignore them
Must experience them
In three dimensional performance
Within their corporeal self
And thus the fate as well
Of those who can't make sense
Of their own communication
Sent with the best intent

We are the ones who distinguish
Pleasure from the pain
Both neurotransmitters
Signals from the brain

We are the ones who judge
Energy to be good or bad
It simply is what it is
Until it makes us sad

Dreams are about emotions
How we feel is all
Wordless communication
Of what in life has stalled

A message to keep moving
And wounds that need to heal
Sometimes we have to act them out
Sometimes the body's killed

And we are freed at last
Of what was holding us back
Illness is a path
Releasing from the past

*

338. Pour Soleil

Mais oui, mademoiselle
Soleil la belle
Un chat de nombreuses couleurs
Les couleurs d'automne
Fourrure douce comme neige
Printemps, elle saute à me
Orbes verts de l'été
Mon amie, Soleil

*

339.

Doubt is a curious thing
The uncertainty of falling water
What it will encounter

Unannounced surprise
Delightful spontaneity
Doesn't want to know ahead of time

Those that choose not to cope
With anything they can't control
Will always judge what they do not know

Those souls full of hope
Will accept the unexpected
As a journey and just go

The water must always fall
The splash transformative
Evaporating mist

This body will break and die
We can choose to control or try
To live with what we find

*

340.

We keep going as if we're getting somewhere
When all there is is joy
The journey has no destination
There is no ending point
The ride is to enjoy

*

341.

Generals of death
Everyone must die
Trust in the cause
Thought lost to emotion
You have to wonder what possessed them
Southern pride ran amuck
Before their fall
Union prevailed because
Right to freedom has a way of winning
Granting mortality its pause

*

342.

The knitting needles weave the blanket
Loop by loop interconnected
One thread can unravel all

Institutions selling fables
People pay for with their lives
Believing til someone cuts the cable

It all works on different levels
It all hurts so many people
To scapegoat with a devil

The ageless play of opposites
That are so much alike
The enemy's a mirror image

We wrap the blanket tight around
Society is sleeping sound
Warmed by ignorance

And once unraveled in its bed
There is no devil—just a thread
Of simple innocence

*

343.

It isn't obsession with death
But its portal
There's no more obvious fact
We are mortal

But even that is temporary
Only our identities
Change in transformation

*

344.

Nobody defragments cities
To make the best use of our space
Because the living do it naturally

Someday our wireless communicating
Will be machine free
No fees and no strings
Simple honesty

*

345.

Buddy who came to visit me often
Offered to share his favorite ball
No complaints and no inhibitions
Gave my friend his all
Over time they will find each other again

*

346.

A pet is a master
That teaches us patience
And kindness and sets priorities
A pet is a gift of compassion
And can unite a family

Pets teach us how
To remember what's important
And how to die with dignity
A pet is a special companion in life
That crosses all cultural boundaries

Pets grieve but go on living
Adapting to what we force on them
Remember to consider their feelings
For they are teachers of compassion
And understand life's meaning

*

347.

Cousins live near Mystic Harbor
Old time town squares
Nearby farmers
Nets bring in fresh lobster
England's settlers founded a home with
Community values
They've kept as their own
I liked the people there
Coastline for sailing and woodland flowers
Under the watch of lighthouse towers
Trace creative invention

*

348.

The simple pleasure of going to sleep
In safety
The joyous adventure of entering dreams
No worries

For all is as it is
There is no should or could be
Resting will give way
To whatever will be

Come what may
I will sleep til I wake
In this life or another

It doesn't matter which it is
Because whichever is will be
And I will sleep til I wake
Safely

*

349.

Life is hard
Too many obstacles
Too many people
Say it must be hard
It must be unpleasant
There can be no reward

Child of the Universe

I want to tell stories
Books with meaning and depth
But the tools required can be enemies
That make me wish that death
Wasn't a revolving door
That leads us to be punished more

I think I should disconnect
Tend my garden
Cuddle my cat
No more email or internet
Communicate by old fashioned letters
Avoid the frustration and bother

I can only see my doctor
If insurance allows it
Because I'm not one of the greedy rich
One needs permission to scratch an itch

Life in the Divided States
We have a right to fear and pain
This is my country
I want it to change

This is the tipping point
Where the spirit breaks
And changes what path it takes

If no one's listening
Why waste words?
Why return?

Franki deMerle

I get tunnel vision
Forget the big picture
Feel disappointment
But life's an adventure
I need to remember
To open my heart

I want my country
To embrace the diverse
Not torture people
Waste time arguing
To make things worse
Too many are homeless

The gift of life
Is laughter and joy
With beauty and paradox
Explore the universe
Within
And enjoy

*

Child of the Universe

350. for Terry

You are the cobra rising up
Not the arrow but the bow
You are triangulation
The tree and the warrior pose

The cobra sways and wraps around
To form Raphael's Caduceus
The Universe's symbol of life
The double helix, the wand of Mercury

The strength of the spine is strung
With the everlasting rainbow
Hope is flexible and sends afar
Cupid's colorful arrows

You are balanced
You are centered
You are the geometry
Of your presence

May your path be peaceful
And filled with the kindly thoughts
Come back around to meet you—
The many you've sent out

*

351.

Mined to death
Over logged
No thought for future generations
The road to the Sun
Always leads away from
No man's land
And open skies lost on closed minds

*

352.

Angels are the in between
Us without the body
Not messengers of the divine
Except as it resides
Within

*

353.

A long time ago
In another land
A friend of mine now
Was my enemy then

We change our roles
We change our bodies
What doesn't change
Is what's inside us

Child of the Universe

My husband in this life
Once long ago
Did terrible deeds
And left me alone

When most in need
Against all I was taught
There was no justice
Found my head on a block

No more victim for me
I must live free
My motto, my motif
Liberty

The eternal point
Of the mystery of life
Is that we can choose
What we do each time

I choose to ignore
Fundamentalist mores
Ignorant of all
But desire to control
I choose not
To play their games
I choose other values
And go my own way

Without delusions forced on us
Manmade religious beliefs
Unnecessary for those who recall
The truth with much relief

Franki deMerle

And my husband in this life
Kept me alive
Injured himself
To save my life

The debt is paid
All is forgiven
We go our own ways
We choose how we live

Eternity encapsulates
A multitude of roles
And turns our view points completely around
Reversal of magnetic poles

Being single suits me now
Time to write and contemplate
Memories saved for lifetimes
Of all that has gone down

Always remember
Never forget
Know who you are
And who you have been
Sometimes the face
Gives itself away
Sometimes it's the ears
The patterns are the same

The instant attraction
That's more than hormones
Is just a reaction
To one you have known

Child of the Universe

Dreams symbolize
Always tell true
On many levels
The essence of you

The pieces are there
If your habit is to search
Put them together
The past can be learned

*

354.

I is for individual
When a person feels alone
And whole
I is for identity
In what ways one is different
Same as every other being

I'm sensitive to the Universe
My origins, where I am
My feelings are important
I have learned to understand
I must say no, enough, no more
When not accepted as I am

I could retreat
But I have a right
To not have to hide
I'm not society's prisoner
I'm a star in the Universe
Here I am

Franki deMerle

I will not back down
Not be shut out
By orthodox exclusivity
I'll not be sucked
Into a black hole
Of rejection and conformity

I stand my ground on galactic dust
As best I dare
To be myself amid the brusque
And harsh insensitive glare
Of the densest mass
Compressing itself into oblivion

I've burned true
My colors shine through
Mass pandemonium
Now I draw a line
That none may cross
And still have privilege of mine

There comes a time when enough is enough
One must define boundaries
The sky is delicately balanced
And environmentally sensitive
Maintain boundaries
To exist safely within fragility

Beauty is fragile
Beauty is random
Beauty is never to be taken for granted
Or put in someone's pigeon hole
Those that ignore it
Suffer from a disease
A symptom of which is stupidity

Child of the Universe

Tread lightly if you would view
The beauty of my world
Respect the sensitive boundaries
For the spectrum to unfurl
The rainbow is a delicate one
It loves the rain, it loves the sun
It needs the roaming eye of awe
To provide appreciation

*

355.

Kindling resentment of diversity
At the heart of a stolen country
Not wanting to know the truth
So much beauty and opportunity
All wasted on false belief
So truly human

*

356. for Joy

You paint what others do not see
Your hands express a mind that's free
But even the earthbound slow
Can only go with the flow

Others see matter
You see energy
Still there is information
In the in between

It permeates us all
Each in their own time
We cannot hurry others
I know—I've tried!

*

357.

Started the blood bath
Over ignorance and foolish pride
Until there was little left
To survive undignified
Hope lies in tolerance and liberal minds

Coastal beaches, swamps and lakes
And military trained to invade
Restitution has yet to be made
Obstinacy stands in the way of
Learning from past mistakes
Intolerance is the biggest delay
Not learning means repeating mistakes
Although compassion is all it takes

*

358.

A world built of façade
That falls apart from time to time
Emotional delusions implode
And I run for my life

But nothing has really changed
Except inside
Shattered by others' false promises
Feels like I died again

Echoes of a lesson unlearned
Direction is only found within
Believing other people's convictions
Only hurts again

The external world is seen
Through the eyes of the soul
Misinterpretation results
In feeling lost and alone

The voice within knows the truth
The voices without babble on
The trick is in shutting them out
Hear the truth from the source and move on

*

359.

Mi guitarra canta
Composiciones del mundo
El más allá
De que yo hablo

La música canta el carácter
De personas históricas
La vida por arte de magia es como
La guitarra yo toco

*

360.

Nimble fingers reaching down
Entering the body of the land
Where touched by an icy hand

Yearning to be free
Old ways persist
Rigid traditions of disharmony
Kindness uplifts

The melting flame that dissipates
Mistrust of differences that once caused hate
Held high by the French lady
Our strength is our diversity

I used to take the subway to New Jersey
Because the rock was hard under my feet
That rock was the island of strength
Where nationalities blend into people

*

Child of the Universe

361.

I have the luxury of illness
To take time for contemplation
It is a well developed habit
A well from which to drink

Those scurrying in all directions
Drive themselves to distractions
That allow the liberty to think
Those moments should be seized upon
To realize the symbolism in
Their choices and actions

Life is far more dreamlike
Than linear literal
The symbols in our waking state
More important than nighttime blurs

We put ourselves in situations
For reasons we'll come to understand
Once we start to see the patterns
That come from our projections
Like movies on a screen
Like holograms dissected and whole

We are more than our individual selves
We are part of so much more
Our stories are allegorical
Parabolic tales but true
The metaphor is you

*

362.

There is so much negative
Bombarding one who's sensitive
It hurts and overwhelms
Makes it hard to function
In this world

The insensitive just don't get it
Have no clue what they create
With petty lies and irritations
That just aren't necessary
They could try to be kind

Maybe they don't realize
All that suffering comes home someday
I wish they'd open their eyes
Look in the mirror and see it coming
Maybe then they wouldn't lie

It's really so unnecessary
All this excruciating caring
For those who just don't care
Or dare to hate for no good reason
The pain they cause stays here

It doesn't count when it's not intended
Where will it all end?
A slate erased—a scale that's balanced
Forgiven
When they forgive

*

Child of the Universe

363.

So much knowledge in the written word
We share all that we learn
Too much bickering in the world
So much writing for translation
Demand for publication
And learning others' wisdom

The pieces of the puzzle fit
So much to learn in reading
An answer needed
May not be in English

So many waste time hating
Thinking they know everything
So afraid of education
My country is divided
By stupidity

Fighting the progressive
They think that generosity
Is bad—how ignorant!
They think that they are moral
While despising liberals
Because they don't believe in dictionaries
Look it up!
No wonder they're afraid of Spanish
They haven't mastered English

One flaw of a democracy
Is that the ignorant vote
Hitler was elected
It could happen here
All it takes is ignorance
And fear

*

364.

Freedom was born here
Reactionary true
Anger channeled toward the cause
Nouveau bleu, blanc et rouge
Casting priorities where they should be
Envisioning the spirit of liberty

Government should be afraid of the people
Not the other way around
Internal values build strength of will
Worldly pleasures are just delights found
In living, in passing turns of the wheel

To know when to stop is a virtue
Without France the USA would not live
They have always told us true
We would be wise to listen
To the best friend of the red, white and blue

True friends do not just go along
With a buddy when they know it is wrong
True friends tell the truth and wait patiently
For their misguided friend to learn through difficulty
Discerning from experience what goes wrong

People are equal
We are all but one race
Economic classes are cruel and misplaced
Ruling by greed is not freedom
People deserve leaders with wisdom

Child of the Universe

This world is such an imperfect place
It's hard enough just to get by day to day
Without having to fight to save face
Without believing in false disgrace
Without being condemned for mistakes

Life should be lived one day at a time
Not projecting one's force onto others
Instead of seeing the truth of one's life
Not being afraid of change for the better
But letting go of control and strife

It's a dream, still a dream
Slowly waking
A massive undertaking
But worth it to flow with the stream
To merge with the oceanic theme

*

Franki deMerle

365. for Pete Bessas

Gentleness should owe no debt
Our world is upside down
When neither doctor nor patient
Have access to profits that abound

You are so much more than doctor
Problem solver and active listener
Dealing with those who suffer
And giving them back their smiles

*

366.

We live in a time of awakening
Many are realizing
Who we are in history
What mistakes we have been making
A time of self discovery

While individuals continue suffering
From what they have forgotten
Searching for recovery
Elusive, frustrating and hidden
Deep in their repressed memory

So many people are afraid
Of what they do not understand
Fear escalates to angry rage
When nothing threatens them
Except their own ignorance

Child of the Universe

Children can't reach emotional maturity
When walled in by repressed memories
No one can teach them to forgive
Until they're ready to let the truth in
And remember what they've forgotten

There is no need for fear
We all get second chances
And however many more
It takes for happenstances
To allow the sore to laugh again

So lighten up
The cosmic dance
Goes on however long we like
Forever is a very long time
In which to get it right

*

367.

Lady Rainbow Goddess
Traveling the sky's night of love
Rabbit dreams of you
Though you're married to the Sun

Your companions skim the lakes
While you control the tides
And in your circling motions
You set the cycle of life

Was it you who hired Ophiucus
To stifle the snake's ego
For boasting to all the other gods
After you gave birth to this world?

Did the Sun know?
Your ever changing form
Silvery wings of light in the night
He slept as it was done

You are a gentle tigress
Prowling the night sky
A sensitive and kind mistress
For the faithful dragonfly

Is it any harder to believe
Than the creation of six days
All we behold born of nothing
From a male having his way

Which is easier to prefer
Which is the more likely
For the act of giving birth—
Man or womankind?

Child of the Universe

Between the archer and the sting
The snake lies penned between
He dares not speak but knows the truth
Not the Sun but the Moon

Dancing above the ocean crests
Flying among the stars
Light reflected in rainbow wings
Of your singing avatars

The surf beats out the rhythm
The wings keep perfect time
And sing the tales of your glory
As you dance across the sky

*

Franki deMerle

368. for Dr. Bernstein

Wisdom and education in combination
How rare for the creative human
Nature needs no schooling

Yet human beings must study
When we've lost our intuition—
Our innate sense of self—

To be human and understand being human
Is wealth
To help another blossom
With natural talent blessed
Is to me your gift

Free to pursue my quest
Without this I had crashed
But thanks to you I'm spared
To save a single life
Is to save the world with care

*

369.

Definitions elude those without vocabulary
Society is made of people interacting
It's called a social network
Who decided socializing was wrong?
Who declared socialism bad?
People working together is all
Any society can ask

Child of the Universe

These are not political thoughts
Just people interacting to give
Opportunities for individuals to excel
And interconnect within
A social network

Who can be afraid of that
With any intelligent gift
To help those on the lower rung of life
Climb the ladder to where they can live
Comfortably

How is helping taking away
Anything but the scourge of poverty
Churches who preach against liberality
Should be fined for preaching against generosity
And scaring people into stupidity

Socialistic means society
That works to take care of its people
Socialism is a value communities
Should learn from progressive education
And strive to imitate

Finding ways to help
Without divisive judging
Helping people help themselves
We all receive by giving

Franki deMerle

I left the Southern Bible Belt
Because of its intolerance
I don't understand fundamentalists
Who teach the fundamentals of ignorance
They simply don't want to admit
They don't have all the answers
No one does but they stand in the way
Of helping those who suffer

The lower class goes to church on Sunday
And believes they should support
The very organizations that take their money
And leave them laboring more
When reading other philosophies
Opens up the mind
We're all just books away
From being free

*

370. for Karen

There is no greater trust
Than to be at one's most vulnerable
No matter what happens next
We have each other

*

371.

Homeless camps behind grocery stores
That disappear at dawn
The working homeless move on

Child of the Universe

Families and individuals
With the fewest resources to pool
The children go off to school

The fortunate still own cars
In which they sleep and move
Until they can no longer afford
The cost of fuel

While fundamentalists with homes
Ignore the illnesses of their own
For brainwashed belief they are God's elite
And do nothing in the face of disease

They are no different from society
That ignores the plight of their own
Believing they are God's elite
While children have no homes

Teachers see them everyday
They cannot focus much less pray
Homework in the dark—no electricity
They don't go to school for education
But to seek shelter
The invisible Americans

When authorities discover where they've been sleeping
They chase them off without safe keeping
While bosses who know provide minimum pay
And go home to their families at the end of the day

This country was founded on killing the nomads
Or relocating them to homeless camps
Nothing much has changed

Franki deMerle

Those of one religion were considered elite
All the rest were savages
Convert or be outcast for eternity
A society that still crucifies
In a country where children are ravaged
Where cruelty is a way of life

Nature is the great equalizer
Floods and mudslides don't know social caste
The rich are as much in danger
Of losing homes as the poor outcasts

And the children are sent to school for a meal
For the present not the future
From this what are they learning?

*

372.

The chains are broken
I am free
The horrific pain is over
And now I breathe

There is no shame that lingers
I did my best and yet
Others under pressure
Were untrue to me

I forgive them and yet
I don't want them back around me
I was let down by a process
War should never be allowed to be

Child of the Universe

I've worked with people in uniform
Good intentions all
But an archaic dysfunctional chaos
That should be allowed no more

Its purpose is to hurt
To humiliate and break
These are not values worth having
They are insidious vices to shake

I once sought
To right wrongs from within
It works within one's soul
Not in organizations

I hope I've learned that lesson
Compromise works only
If there is honesty in both parties
Then the result is true

But when deceit arrives
Honesty has left the stage
The only result of deceptive play
One is betrayed, enslaved

The more people that are involved
The more they all must listen
And counter and expose the lies
For the sake of millions

I hope I'm done with uniforms
And machines of war
And religions based on human lies
I desire their presence no more

My chains are broken
I am free
They've no right to judge me
Mock me or rank me

I am done
With artificial protocols
And emotional vampires
Building imprisoning walls

I don't need a fortress in the stars
No threat assessment or safety plan
I'm free of my fetters
Though killed I still am

*

373. for Arnetta

You restored my sanity
In the midst of madness
You convinced me I wasn't crazy
I miss your calm common sense
Your appropriate indignation
And your laugh

But mostly I appreciate the sweaters
The flannel and leather jackets
Cause girlfriend it gets cold up here
In the Great Northwest
Whoever named the Pacific Ocean was nuts
Or a poet

*

Child of the Universe

374.

Depression begins in repression
Its roots are tangled deep
And weave a net of confusion
That interrupts one's sleep

It produces intolerable pain
What's given returns threefold
Never stifle another's expression
Their story must be told

My mother denied me myself
I found me anyway
But she died a dreadful death
Of all her memories

It wasn't at all about me
Certainly not from her perspective
Humans are strings all tangled up
Untangled by compassion

Habit sets the pattern
Redundancy by nature
Kinks and knots can be unraveled
By a kind demeanor

Repression begins in fear
People hurt each other so
Sometimes it's such a habit
That they no longer know

The pain they cause which will return
To wake them from their daze
The wake up call that breaks the pattern
And offers the path to change

*

375.

You came to me at a crucial time
The color of your past death
To let me know what was happening
To give me the connection
Between the now and then

The karma that unfolds sometimes
Is better understood
When put in context of its origins
To see the loose ends
Come together retied

Yes it happens
A soul reaches through from the past
In a dream
Through that medium
We cannot define

Matter, energy and information
Coexist in time
So that there is no event
For which we cannot find
An explanation

Why is it to the vain
Beauty in others is a crime?
How selfish are they
Who would blame another
For Nature's kindness shining

Child of the Universe

And yet it happened to us
Jealousy confounded
What should have been pure love
Hatred by others compounded
A couple's troubles

And so you came to me
When we came around full circle
And helped me rise above
And understand just what
Was soon to come

All these years I'd wondered
You came out of the blue
As if you meant to rescue
Someone you once knew
I still love you too

*

376.

I'm not the saint that nurses the sick
Or feeds the hungry or saves the poor
I only offer thoughts and words
And hope consolation is found
Somewhere on this hardship path
Where suffering abounds

My work is in the details
I do what little I can
To weave the strands together
So that someone understands

Understanding is the battle
Epiphany sets the course
We only have to follow
The understanding of our hearts

*

377.

Ice, the crystalline beauty
To glide across is to fly
When melted permeates all life
But frozen beautifies

Reminds how crystals intertwine
Water molecules blend together
All life depends on all other life
We must protect the Earth

Change in climate and weather
So many species are gone
Populations gather together
In cities of concrete and iron

But Nature has the final say
The justice scales are hers
The ice provides the place for play
The balance is the skater's

*

378.

I live in a time when rappers
Use rhythm and rhyme to vent
When poetic verse
Sparks the mysteries' glint
A melodic line of thought
Considers inner space
While timeless profanities
Shout right in my face

I fear the lack of consideration
Is the lack of meaningful education
Some chase sensuality to fill the void
Others feel internal energy coil
And see the patterns everywhere
Of intelligent information's stare

Daring one to step inside
A world where pride is senseless
Emotions are instinctive guides
To what is pre-self-evident
The journey of personal discovery
Has no final destination
External shallow prattling
Ends in neural constipation

*

Child of the Universe

379. for John B

Dear John I am sorry
I don't care for the swamps of Wisconsin
But still there is beauty—Hot diggity!
And cranberries!

It doesn't matter where one lives
You make even swamp sound inviting
It's nice to be appreciated
Hot diggity! it's enticing

Love is the gravity of mass
The stuff that bends starlight
I'd write if I had your address
But I wouldn't spend the night

You figured that out—Hot diggity!
Still nothing has gone wrong
I found a way to be happy and safe
And write my special song—no regrets

The point is there is always an answer
We must listen and we must wait
But whenever we ask a question
An answer comes back someday

*

380.

Simple is enlightenment
It grows from a little seed
That germinates from habit

The seed is just a thought
Its comfort nourishes
So it will be repeated

And repeated enough times
The thought becomes a habit
That slowly sheds the light

A seed is a tiny package
Surrounded by nourishment
Until its food exhausted

It's forced to germinate
And seek what is its habit
Or it will terminate

Everything starts over
Matter, energy, thought
Nothing is ever over

One simple repeated thought
Becomes a habit
One simple desire is sought

Habit becomes a practice
Part of one's routine
A way of seeking solace

Child of the Universe

If the practice is discarded
The thought becomes unconscious
And waits where ways have parted

Until the need arises
In yearning for lost comfort
The thought appears to guide us

Back to habit and to practice
To the path that leads to light
Back to the solace of kindness

Some wish for the end of time
So they don't have to practice
They've made it so hard in their minds

But it's so simple
We've infinite lives
And no excuses

So back to the thought and the practice
To the path that shines the light
Back to the solace of kindness

*

381.

I like to think I'm progressing
As I pass the years
I like to think I'm getting better
At sharing what is dear

I have not lost the ability
To appreciate simplicity
And wonder at the complexity
Of this creative ploy

For we have wakened to the truth
What happens to us is what we choose
By how we think and perceive
And what we will to dream

We are part of the process
A big responsibility
To choose what one will wish
Once one acknowledges reality

The gift of free will means
No deity will interfere
With the exercise of dreams
And what we cause to appear

There's no one else to blame
We do all to ourselves
Before we accept acclaim
Let's make sure we wish ALL well

*

Child of the Universe

382. for Elizabeth

You are the puzzle lady
Who gives to each a piece
That interlocks with mysteries
We hold all inside
And delineate the memories
We chose to put aside
Because we could not see the place or time
From which they hide

You're the facilitator
That opens up the door
So we may dare to venture down
To what we've lived before
The feel of clothes upon the skin
The closeness of the walls within
The food we ate and type of plate
To put the puzzle piece in place

I learned why I must write
Determined to have my say
Even when men will never listen
As long as I have ink and paper
My words will find a way
To be heard
Society is cruel and strange
I'll not defer

*

Franki deMerle

383.

The crashes come more frequently now
The world is an unstable place
It shatters far more easily now
Like it's made of brittle lace

My rhythms are much less intricate
I seek simplicity
My being is much more delicate
I just need to be believed

I am grateful for not being alone
My life is graced with love
I appreciate having a pleasant home
I am fortunate enough

Still the poet's curse is seen
It visits more and more
No matter thought or philosophy
Depression is at the door

It's not for lack of trying
I cannot shake its hold
I spend too much time crying
Over things I can't control

Some say don't take it personally
But what in life is not?
I am a creature of feelings
Turn them off? I will not!

My feelings make me who I am
My sensitivity
Has shaped this very woman
Who hurts at what she sees

Child of the Universe

A world of pain and suffering
Where people with an income
Would deny medical relief
To those without a home

My country boasts of greatness
Based on military strength
While education languishes
In superstitious belief

We all have opportunities
To learn or repeat mistakes
It's sad to see when many
Have only greed to take

I feel most for the children
I fear being one again
They see it all but have no say
In what they will inherit

On my best days my sense of awe
Carries me on its wings
But it cannot protect me from
The inevitable shattering

*

384.

Kindle what feels right
In awareness we are one
No need to cling or fight
Deeds speak the mind as song
Nothing means more than the thought
Essentially intentions are might
So wish all loving kindness
Simple thought brings forth the light

*

385.

The Buddha ordained no clergy
Jesus ordained no pope
Mohammed and Moses only wrote the rules
To quiet unruly groups

Krishna talked of duty
To emphasize a point
But he never said that war
Should be a way of life

It comes down to each person
To decide how to live a life
Power is a waste of time
No one controls the mind

Except the individual
Who chooses what to think
Never give away that power
Because you still must keep

Child of the Universe

Responsibility
Leaders unenlightened
Will ask for your money first
And then for blind allegiance

Any time you pay someone
They rightly work for you
Don't let them tell you what to think
It is your duty to choose

And if they do not keep their word
Or try to change your mind
Fire them and wish them well
You'll meet another time

Some think they must control the world
They're afraid of what's inside
Which is of course where to find true work
To try to tame the mind

No need to bother with wandering thoughts
Just practice taking time
To send the thought of kindness
Simplicity reigns sublime

You don't need a teacher
Many have passed this way
You only need to make the choice
Let habit rewire your brain

As long as you can think the thought
As long as you can try
The light will find you where you are
And kindness will fill your mind

*

386.

It's a choice
What to do with time
It's a voice
That speaks to the collective mind
It's individuals
Who ultimately decide
It's free will
That follows the heart as its guide
It's brilliance
That knows no wrong or right
It's enlightenment
Once you realize

*

Child of the Universe

387.

I have little energy left
So what I have left I'll share
May you be free from suffering
May you always know I care

Anger is only natural
Direct it only at its source
It will always spend itself
Love is the eternal force

Words spoken and written down
Are thoughts shared and carried on
They echo in the heart
Where the only true meaning is found

There is no literal directive
There are no laws that must stand
And no eternal judgment
There's only a choice to intend

So may you be at ease
With your body and your thoughts
And may you always feel at peace
With all that you have wrought

*

388. for Kathy D

You are a traveler of the mind
There are places you know how to find
That elude others

This is a special present
From the Universe
Because you are protective
Of this Earth

*

389.

Reset to default positions
Wipe the circuit board clean
Of any misinstructions
Time to make a clean sweep

Shut down the conscious mind
Give the brain a rest
A chance to restore and energize
A chance to be reset

And once the switch flips on
Leave all the garbage behind
Starting over as just oneself
The Universe connects with Mind

*

390. for Dawn

Your name is native to this land
Your face the light of day
Your healing gift flows through your hands
As you feel your way

Helping others is a gift
Your smile just magnifies
I am so glad I met you
You truly are de Light

*

391.

I get impatient with selfishness
Greed and stupidity
I don't understand what others are thinking
When they're only thinking of themselves
I get impatient with myself

It's hard to let go sometimes
The big picture is not always clear
When I forget to stop and listen
With my inner ear
To my own spirit

But feelings arise from inside
Feelings that are usually right
That somehow manage to guide
My actions, words and writing
Back into the light

Depression is anger internalized
Fighting to express what's wrong
When what I see around me is crying out
For someone to verbalize
How much everyone feels alone

*

392. for Cam

The camera's eye sees the reality
The artist paints what is true
You are on the path of enlightenment
The kindness and beauty that are you

*

393.

Communism died
Capitalism failed
Slavery of the poor by the rich
Is a definition of hell

I'm done with this shameful circus
No more military
No more lies
No more politics of any kind
I have a life

This ship is sinking
This is where I get off
Everyone for themselves
And all for One
Therein lies the hope

Child of the Universe

I have my own path
I have my own dance
To a cosmic rhythm
That's not by chance

Let go the insane
Laugh at the inane
But don't think for one moment
I owe you anything

We enter life alone
We exit single file
Not to a grotesque judgment
But to rise above the guile
And reassess

Why wait?
My agenda is my own
I can come through this unscathed
No debate
I'm staying close to home

For safety
For inner peace
For inner guidance only I can find
I have my own lofty dreams
I decide the use of my time

*

394.

Someone once coined the phrase
"Random acts of kindness
And senseless beauty"
Someone gave the world a blessing
It was very much in need of

I once saw graffiti on a garbage can
You are what you hate
It made a difference
It made me expand
It's important not to hate

It's so hard to not be angry
At those who abuse the vulnerable
I express my anger internally
And abuse the vulnerable me
And hate my very essence
Abuse my sensitivity perceives

The only cure is kindness
Found in inner beauty
That serves no other purpose
Than to set a person free

*

395. for Celia

You are a guardian angel
Of the children of the Goddess Bast
You are a lady in waiting
To the royal kingdom of cats

*

396.

Memories are all we have
To tie us to our past
Yet through them we unleash deceit
Intended to protect
Our conscious minds from everything
Our egos would detest
Despite the truth that could be had
To learn our soul's behest
And so we share experience
But never same perspective
Together in the same place and time
In individual bubbles
Because of this constant trick of mind
We cause ourselves such troubles
All for pride in what's not real
Perception creates individuals

*

397.

Robin, sweet bird of song
You must take care of yourself first
You must keep yourself strong
To give to others

You have the future
Enjoy your journey
The gift to yourself
Will be your discovery

*

Franki deMerle

398.

Look at the space in which you live
To know who you are and who you have been
Then let go and transcend

Sensation is not good or bad
Tides of emotions are governed by thoughts
If you don't judge you can float

The mind works by habit
Reinforced by practice
That's all it is

Don't judge
Let go
It just is

But after all that's been said
Has the laundry been done?
Has the porch been swept?

*

Child of the Universe

399.

If you don't know the cause of illness
All you can do is just treat the symptoms
Exploring the past is a meaningful experience
To understand the mirror's reflection

Blind acceptance of others' beliefs
That you've never lived before
Eliminates the possibilities
That your suffering can be cured

We look to the past to improve the future
And understand the present
Why we fear what we fear and why we are here
Comes from experience—but we must remember

In learning we move to the center hub
In ignoring we ride the rim
The wheel keeps on turning regardless what's done
Location, location, location

*

400. for Gayle

You have the patience of eternity
You would not have survived otherwise
You have the strength of the military
And the steadiness of the tides

You have the gift of mothering
You use it all the time
Your charges entrusted by Mother Nature
Are blessed you are so kind

*

401.

The flag of peace passed to the messenger
Became a symbol of health
Why is it now this country
Shoots the messenger and steals the wealth?

The flag of peace, the dawn of hope
Obscured by smoke of gunfire
Stolen by a military coup
And most seem unaware

We are a country of lost memories
Destined to repeat
All we've failed to overcome
Blocks the way and lies at our feet

A nation that refuses to adapt to truth
Is a nation that's doomed to fail
I am not willing to accept that doom
If compassion can prevail

*

Child of the Universe

402.

Remembering is a blessing
It allows me to understand
Why I've been through all I have

I now have the freedom
To choose to be free of the past
Choices made of delusion

I have nothing left to prove
To others who think they have the answers
Except that I can learn kindness

No one can control others
There is no real, true power
Except kindness

Wasting time with right and wrong
Is thinking you are the judge of all
It always leads to your downfall

I now begin the journey again
This time with remembering
And when considering options
Asking which is kindest

*

Franki deMerle

403. for Marla

A healer and a dancer
Eurynome of old
When that male snake stole her credit
She kicked his teeth out cold

You are the serpent holder
Misnamed by boastful men
Denying the power of our gender
Set them straight again!

*

404.

Others see who they want us to be
Or what they don't like about themselves
Both require judgment of values
Both should be drenched in doubt

But we so rarely question our judgment
So accustomed we are to believing we must have it
We judge out of fear, we judge without thinking
We judge out of habit

I've missed the truth of so many beings
By not taking control of what I was thinking
Stopping and seeing real human people
In their own glow of beauty

Sometimes it's best to listen to feelings
That come from much deeper within
Than the shallow thoughts of the waking brain
That interferes with perceiving what is

*

405.

I have a habit of seeking out men
Who want to be mothered like children
It's a habit I intend to break
If they don't stand on their own two feet
I will
And I will leave them

No more smothering kudzu
No more ivy clinging to my legs
Show me a man that can bloom
And stay within his own space

Sex may be physical pleasure
Or an expression of amazing grace
It's a choice both partners should agree on
Before it ever takes place

Always during orgasm
Honesty shows one's true face
But be careful of projected feelings
That mirror you in the other's place

*

406.

For so long men have taught that women
Only have value in raising of children
Childhood should be finished as quickly as possible
To begin living

Parents that want to hold back their young
Prevent them from seeing the world whence they're born
Are just control hungry
And unhappy with fun

We are who we are
We each have our own path
You cannot control others
That's just fact

Women have lives and choices to make
With or without men
Or children to raise
That's how it is

If you don't like the schedule
Someone's forced upon you
Just walk away
To your own path stay true

If you lack your direction
Ask til the answer is clear
But consider your sources
Before acting on what you hear

Child of the Universe

The only truth you can verify
Is what your own heart holds inside
Never somebody else's rules
Best to find your own hidden jewels

There's no wisdom another can teach
You can only learn
What you already have
Within your own reach

And herein is my parenting
To the youth of the world
Empty promises aren't real
Others' dogma isn't you

*

Franki deMerle

407.

I worked with the French Resistance
Smuggled radio parts sewn into toys
Got caught, was shot
Died in an oven
Can't put it any plainer than that
I live

Jack London was massacred
Many writers have told their own tales
The world seems oblivious to the obvious
But if one person listens
We haven't failed

Now in the Age of Aquarius
The truth at last comes out
Though ever present clouds of darkness
Always try to wipe us out
We come back
We find the clues we left for ourselves
Uncover and reveal the past

*

Child of the Universe

408. for Joel

You have your life ahead of you
And many lives behind
You don't make the same mistake twice
In that you are already wise

Always base your decisions
On your own experience
And intuition

Follow your dreams
Waking and sleeping
And know we all love you

*

Franki deMerle

409.

Groups that proclaim they are universal
Have at their core their own survival
Wherever you go there are people
And someone will muck it all up

It's true of all good intentions
Because they focus on how good they are
Many would call me a cynic
But fantasy only carries so far

I'd rather be honest than nice
I'd rather be alone in the night
Without the anxiety of promises unkept
By good intentions and actions that never met

I love my solitude in the night
No jabber or clamor from elsewhere
Just face time with reflective introspection
And insights not found elsewhere

I'm responsible for my survival
Free to give as I please
Where compassion says there is a need
Rather than organizational greed

*

410.

Greatness is only within the message
All messengers risk their lives
Bringing out the truth
Realizing all the lies are found
In our delusions
Epiphanies are everywhere
Lilies' fragrance and beauty random

Open the door to kindness
Unleash the messenger's voice
Expect the unexpected joy
Stillness and listening supply
The mercy of a purposeful life

Water is the essence
All life depends upon
The feelings deep within that guide
Emotions symbolized
Reveal the inner you

*

411.

Physical pain unrelated
To serious illness or injury
Can be mitigated
By exercise

Emotional pain is similar
If not the same
Doing something of beauty
Will bring a smile to a face

A smile is a thing of beauty
That goes on forever when seen
Others find it contagious
Ad infinitum—to eternity

*

412.

May all people everywhere find
Always a way to share
Yesterday is a lesson

All we need to do is
Learn from it and
Let it go

Child of the Universe

Best not to seek revenge
Everything comes home
I know this from experience
No harm intended
Grows
Simple kindness
Beauty inspires and
Everyone breathes deep

How many seek false rules
And judgments to lead the way
Peace is not found in "thou shalt not's
People are individual jewels
Yet so many shine unnoticed

Perception leads to gratitude of
Eternity's Universe
All around diversity
Compares none to the worst
Each of us full of worth
For wonder of the moment
Understands all that is and
Lets the Universe in

Force knows to flow around
Resistance throws itself away
Each has the choice of fight or flight
Each can just walk away

Finding one's own balance
Requires hearing the inner voice
Of guidance, conscience and kindness
Masked by thoughts of malice and pain of sacrifice

Franki deMerle

Sensationalism is distraction
Until we learn to listen
From within
From our heart of kindness
Everything is what it is
Repeating lessons we have yet to learn
In a circle of life and death
Newness a delusion
Great wheel always turns

All of us on our very own paths
None of us without options
Decisions are how we travel
Attached to the rim or
Toward the center

Each kindness helps another
And comes home again
So kindness is the way to go
Eternity weaves what we spin

*

413.

Some don't want to know what's wrong
Their feelings are overloaded
But what seems nice can also be wrong
This feeling thing is complicated

Truth isn't always pretty
But you can't always identify
A problem blindly, subjectively
When you look for beauty in lies

There is always beauty in truth
Hidden deeply and hard to find
But the idealism of youth
Gives way to open eyes

*

414.

La vida es buena
Cuando no hay dolor
A veces solo una sonrisa
Es suficiente para ayudar
A olvidar su dolor
Por un momento

*

415.

Much time is wasted redefining
And trying to get somewhere
Much time is wasted seeking purpose
When it is being here

*

416.

I find the gloom of minutia
The ugliness fixated upon
To drain my joyful essence
I find it to be so wrong

To dampen others' spirits
With hate and prejudice
Is either sin or sickness
And I must strongly protest

Child of the Universe

A boundary must be set
The perimeter patrolled
To not let the hatred others covet
Permeate uncontrolled

When I say "no" I mean it
When asked to stop some persist
They must be cut off and not allowed
To intrude upon my quest

I must not be influenced
By those whose hearts are cold
To not be kind to animals
So willing to cuddle and hold

So many pets domesticated
Are wiser by far than I
Wordless their clear example
Provides a truer guide

*

417.

Idealism does not contradict realism
Greed and profits are fantasies
Victory in war cannot be achieved
Only helping living beings
Brings the peace we seek

*

418.

We live in the age of pushing buttons
No wound is allowed to heal
No nerve remains not stepped on
You're resented if you feel

Yet everyone expresses an opinion
Everyone is cyber talking
But no one listens
Contradicting voices are blended

Families are the worst at it
Ignoring your skills and experience
Interrupting, contradicting and shouting you down
When you're just trying to make some sense

A sibling raised to be the victim
When another has a true handicap
Cannot be explained by the parents
Who suffer from memory gap

Some see clearly
Others stumble with a crutch
I remember my experiences
But others claim to know so much

So many anomalies
In human behavior
Defy explanation
By present day standards

We come into this world for the presence
We become who we are
From experience
No one else, of course, respects it

Child of the Universe

And all the jibber jabber
Of gossip and false pride
Leaves me seeking silence
Can't get a word in edgewise

As a child I learned to hide
Or face the scapegoat lies
Some still brush me aside
And ignore what I've learned in life

So I will learn eventually
Not to try to tell them
Let them make their own mistakes
Even if it kills them

This is after all one of many
There is no compassion in judging
There is no redemption in belief
Only doing

The family forms a basic lesson
And frames experiences to come
The true family is the Universe
We are never and always at home

The perpetual victim with a faulty memory
The passive aggressive diva of façade
The controlling paranoid narcissist
Have left the rest of us depressed

My impulse was to run away
Into the arms of a man who once raped me
Many lifetimes ago
In that one he was my downfall

Franki deMerle

I would not have gone with him otherwise
But he charmed me with his truth and lies
Such is the nature of romance
And danger hides behind the chance

To be loved at last
To be wanted for oneself
To believe that it can all work out
To finally find encouragement

The search for confidence
The courage not to hide
While all the time in private
I write

I worked for years to get anger out
Because I didn't deserve it aimed at myself
Anger internalized can snuff a life out
But suicides are a painful way out
For everyone

The problem is all the judging
And not wanting to hear alternate views
The problem is thinking we know everything
And one's just an appendage to lose

So now I speak out
I call others on it
I get the feelings out
And of course they don't like it

Child of the Universe

But I prefer their upset
To being flattened by steam rollers
I choose to not be a victim
I choose not to be wounded

Some would rather perhaps
I stayed quiet and hid
Like in the days of old
When I'd no reason to live

Some may not like the way my feelings come out
But it's up to me to take my side
And I've learned to direct anger at the cause
Rather than run and hide

When I look at the bigger picture
I see just how funny I am
Humans can be so silly
I look in the mirror and laugh

Arguments end in a laugh
Enemies become friends
Lovers struggle and hurt each other
Only to love again

We take ourselves so seriously
One moment we're here then we're dead
We obsess about safety and security
And loose the moment instead

They say the truth hurts and it's true
Pushes a button, steps on a nerve
You've always denied was there
And it hurts but it's true

Franki deMerle

Me—I'd rather die laughing
At my own inconsistencies
No matter the day's death toll
The birds of the air still take wing

And I wonder about this bonding process
That happens only with pets and men—
That parents choose to love certain offspring
And disregard the rest

And what reason for being rejected
Unless to not linger too long
And move on somewhere else when it's over
To a family in tune with one's song

The next generation is sadly in pain
From the same type of prejudicial practice
Some are loved
And some abandoned

And parents move on as if the problem
Has already resolved
But the feelings must surface
Like a boil that must burst

Even though no one likes it
The poisonous rejection must explode
Preferably in the direction of the source
And relieve the sufferer of the load

There is no rational adult talk
In situations like these
There are no rational adults at all
Bandaids versus psychology

Child of the Universe

Only children are truly free
To react with honest feelings
Then there are emotional adults
The rest stuck in the state of seriously

It is the true health crisis
All this seriousness tenses
All the problems humans create
Lost in a world full of hate

And the ever widening gulf
That I cross as I leave to find myself
Someday I will disconnect the buttons
And free myself

*

419.

Balanced like a razor's edge
Blade upon the ice
Balanced day to day to dredge
Through tension of daily life
Weaving through the ruckus
To look back and find meaning
In the etching of our patterns
Poised to cut through the surface
So smoothly, beautifully clean
To the danger of the depths
Where our true feelings face us
The origins of our dreams

*

420.

We are the enemy
A country based on military
Ravaging the poor
And claiming to be terrorized

But look into the eyes
Of those fighting back
See the mirrored image
Of the compassion we lack

*

421.

Life is a work in progress
The beauty and the pain
Some choices labeled mistakes
For fear of shame

The hard parts are the unhealed wounds
We hide as ugliness
Though they are treatable with truth
We do not like to face
For fear of shame

It's not about religious difference
It's not about political disagreement
It's about not recognizing
They are like us
And all fear shame

*

Child of the Universe

422.

Delusion imagines states of perfection
In unrealistic stasis
Nowhere found in Nature
Simply doesn't exist

We have imagination
As fertile as our dreams
The diversity of galaxies
Vast as life in the seas

Yet some use their minds
Amassing property
And others find themselves
In squalid poverty

The problem with perception
Is the illusion of time
That slows or moves too quickly
Along adrenal lines

Our minds are no longer limited
By where our brains have come to be
Trying to redefine
What is social normalcy

Judgment of what's right
Evolves now day to day
Judgment leaves no room
For innocence at play

Right and wrong box in
And limit possibility
Where compassion finds a way
Toward constructive understanding

Franki deMerle

But everything we've known so far
Comes simply down to money—
Which is valued over life—
Which is still considered property

Because our minds are so much more
Than the brains we have evolved
We must use the grey creatively
For poverty to dissolve

And find a way to reintroduce
Kindness to the controlling
To protect them from their rage and fear
In a time stream ever flowing

The spectrum is infinity
Of colors beyond what we can see
The black and white solutions
Are as fragile as glass on concrete

Because it's not about "me"
Compassion is funny that way
Nobody ever stays the same
All life is funny that way

All pain is temporary
As is everything
If something makes you worry
Just wait—it's sure to change

*

Child of the Universe

423.

Some seek the placid water
For peace, stillness and calm
I prefer the rhythmic waves
And wake of motor boats gone
The motion is a healing balm

I'm not afraid to capsize
I wear a vest that floats
The land is thick and still and dense
The water never so
It holds emotions of the depths

I do not fear the water
In its liquid or crystalline states
It comforts me with rocking
I fly while on my skates
It comprises most of my body

I do not fear my being
I am a work of art
Created by Mother Nature
Not to be set apart
But to appreciate her comforts

*

Franki deMerle

424.

Disappointment is an indication
Of a symbol we have lost
An idea of ourselves we thought was permanent
But was not

The pattern of attachment
Begins before our birth
With fear and anticipation
Of what we will be worth

And by joy or disappointment
That greets us once we're here
We learn to choose a safety zone
For attachments without fear

I project acceptance
Upon inanimate things
Because there's no rejection
Like relationships bring

Others find their own way
To compensate for blows they were dealt
Like controlling and isolating loved ones
Or pretending all is well

The point is where attachment lies
Is always a minefield
Where others unknowingly violate
Every comfort that you feel

And then they'll say you overreacted
To having been violated
All you can do when your world is shattered
Is try your best to explain it

Child of the Universe

But everyone has a breaking point
At which they must withdraw
Because they simply don't have to defend
Being here at all

Life is violent and chaotic
And comfort zones must be defined
Always know and patrol the boundary
To protect your safety line

*

425.

Someone asked me once
What I wanted to be
My answer was simple and flippant
To have the wisdom of a yogi
To share through writing

Be careful what you ask for
It may just come to pass
The wisdom I have found
Is all my weaknesses
And how I have created them
While thinking I was the victim

But I will keep my end of it
And not hold back my pen
I'll tell the truth and the whole of it
And then begin again

For truth has many levels
Like layers in the rock
Nature holds us accountable
For what we claim we forgot

I can deny with the best
What lies in what I've written
And still be proud to own my worst
For Nature made me human

*

426.

The petals open slowly
Floral tenderness
Botanical sexuality
Exposing inner essence

Child of the Universe

All the plant can be
Its wholeness, its completeness
On display to be seen
It knows no inhibitions

This is true accomplishment
The essence of integrity
Recognition shared that moment
Faults turned into beauty

By honesty
Seeing past the past
Into possibility
Answers to questions asked

The willingness to unfold
The petals of personality
To see, to know, to own

And take responsibility
Releases all the tension
Of stressors kept too long
Let go as in an orgasm
One's truth exposed to all

This is the moment of greatness
That Nature did intend
To know and own one's weakness
With nothing to defend

This is the ultimate tenderness
Revealed as epiphany
When one and all know one's true self
And celebrate its beauty

Franki deMerle

The moment bears forgiveness
As a crown of glory
To wear in self awareness
The truth of one's own story

*

427.

People do not fear the truth
What they fear is shame
They fear that all their deeds and words
Echo from their name

They fear to be judged lesser
Than the innocence of Nature
Which sees them only as they are
And all that they have learned

*

Child of the Universe

428.

The petals float on water
Soft and silky loam
Fluidity of foam

The color catches the eye
Fire without the smoke
The blaze of burning hope

The petals rest upon the stem
They are the crowning dome
Upon a transient home

The petals float on air
Sweet scent fills the nose
The aroma of a rose

A home is not a place
A true home is a space
Filled with one's own soul

*

429.

I write for those who would understand
For those who don't want to judge
It is in words I make my stand
I hope none hold a grudge

For that would be self defeating
The point is just to laugh
To many I am a foolish clown
For me that is enough

I've learned to get around this Earth
And stand my higher ground
For some it's been important
To think I have backed down

But they deceive themselves
These words will be around
When we have passed to other realms
These words will still resound

*

430.

Life is so hard for the wealthy
So much money to manage
Tasks to delegate
Not understanding what really
It takes to make things happen

We of the lower classes
Must not be too quick
To enable them with our sympathy
To continue to expect
Entitlement

And oh the burden they bear
Of paying their fair taxes
In community service
No, must not be too quick to judge
What luxuries must be abandoned

*

431.

I'm better off a recluse
No one helps the honest poor
Except each other
The bitterness continues

Our captain steals a prize for peace
With bloody hands does not release
Government is folly
Why can't they see the light?
Why must they fight?

I'm ashamed to live in a warring nation
Military destroys civilization
The violence always comes home

It's a sad state of affairs
When peaceful people have no heirs
No one to joy in life and Earth
And love what is simply there

*

432. for Aife and Barbara

You have so mistaken me
A compliment no doubt
Intended but not understood
A fog engulfing cloud

For I was much abducted
But not for slavery
Nor have I ever chosen
To return so quickly
You flatter me in searching
Perhaps you see the One
That hides divine in each of us
Light brighter than the Sun

*

433.

Welcome to our world
This is hell
It gets better or worse
Depending on how you feel
Make no mistake
This is hell

When conscience overcomes us
And plagues our minds with guilt
We are in Purgatory
We have the choice to quit
And return to victim status
Unless we can forgive

Child of the Universe

Freedom from all judgment
Is Paradise indeed
Rare to find a soul who dwells
In such a lofty creed
But it is real
Heaven is in deed

None have anything to do
With what others say is so
Everything is written in the heart
The only streets paved with gold
Or melted down into flame
Are within the same

We decide who we will be
Or are or who we've been
There are no prophets among men
But for women's intuition
Leaders must now step aside
For free interpretation

Information overload
Has doomed morality
To struggling in the deepest bog
Trying to get free
It's up to those who aren't bogged down
To live in liberty

*

434.

Life itself has no titles
Society names its days
That no longer have a meaning
Except in work and play
We give each thing a name
But what is it we call
This or that particular phase
Of life we've lived beyond?

Titles are for aristocracy
To wear with put on airs
The name we carry to the grave
Will fade and decay there

While just a word on one last breath
Is carried on the wind
Of spirit long surviving death
Blown where it lives again

Illumined by the inner light
It guides us from within
While parents choose a stranger's name
Unknowing where we've been

*

Child of the Universe

435. for Molly P

You know me well
As a precious animal
Needing only to be loved

Abandoned by its mother
Or somehow separated
Desperate for touch

Once I shied from human contact
Fearful its deceit
Was just too much

And now beyond that grave
The fear has long been killed
By desire to feel

Be careful what you wish
Lest you receive too much
The pain unbearable

But here I am again
Half wit? maybe so
But what secrets I reveal

*

436.

Each of us choose what we are part of
A family, a country
A flock of doves
The planet or Universe
United as One

*

Franki deMerle

437.

He said I didn't flirt
Then what are all these words?
I separate myself in space and time
From what may hurt

There is a man who still lays claim
To my heart
And when we touch in flesh again
I hope I'm smart
Enough to know his weakness—
Pride is not the worst
But cannot hide
The jealous dark

I've been his muse in dreams
A lovely voice—he sings
Of which we spoke
But still I know
How used I've been
When all I wanted
Was a friend

Forgiveness will not come
Until we meet again
And for once I see
Truth of the man
Women who are wise
Will understand

I love a peacock
The colors, not the strut
So many eyes
To see into the heart

*

Child of the Universe

438.

Now I see the fallacy
Of wanting a man to rescue me
From what I have become

Some call it crush or obsession
It was really self deception
But I must be free

You have to stand on your own two feet
You have to hold your own end up
You cannot lean

There is no fairy tale in love
Only fairy wings
That must work hard to keep the beat

Partnership is equality
And equal responsibility
Love sonnets fail miserably

*

Franki deMerle

439. for Marvin Bell

Yes there is eternity
And we yet again may meet
I'd like that very much

White is the sum of all colors
The Sun is the sum of summers
It's all about the light

And I do love heights
To view the panorama
As if upon bird's flight

Find me in the highlands
Where slanted rains shower
We can meet there then

*

440.

To some I am an oddity
An open book to read
And still not comprehend—
They only know convention

I'll have none of it
I'm free to be childlike
While seeing false priorities
And laughing at them

And I don't hold back
When I have something to say
Especially when someone else is hurt
By the petty games being played

Child of the Universe

What they've missed is simple—
No hidden agenda here
Only happy in creativity
And trying to be fair

Silence is not a woman's place
Wisdom is ours to be discovered
While men are busy saving face
We are the truth givers

I don't have time for egos
Expecting catering
I have better things to do—you know
I must have time for writing

Because I will have my say
Because I have things to say
I won't surrender to anyone
I won't do it any other way

It's who I am for a reason
And I'm moving on from here
I will not be a victim again
Be intimidated or live in fear

It's mine to choose
My life to live
My life, my rules
Maybe they'll forgive

*

441. For Richard Wilbur

I love to be up in the trees
With the birds I feel at ease
I fly above them in my dreams
Higher than the high rises
Out among the stars
I thought to be an astronaut
Of light instead of fire

So many restrictions and obstacles
Unmovable unlike in dreams
But climbing up above it all
Restores the reality
That even in this troubled world
We are free

We're bound in life by gravity
But it cannot capture dreams
And when time comes that we must leave
We only take our dreams

*

442.

It's a nation of chemical dependence
With a history of substance abuse
Playing out all the symptoms
And violence on the stage of the world

We imprison a third of the country
And campaign for more police
Who are convicted of corruption
We're only seeking release

Child of the Universe

When the prisoners outnumber the free
Will anyone be left
For pity, for empathy—
To supply the medicine we need?

What are we doing, people?
Are we so afraid
We have forgotten how to live?
So much for the home of the brave

Society is a social being
Democracy doesn't have to be antisocial
Being liberal denotes generosity
And being socialist is all about people

Human beings have sought remedies
Ever since they evolved
In harmony with the plant kingdom
Accepting that pain can be solved

But now it's owned by CEOs
With excessive profits and bonuses
They want to own our very lives
It's all about greed and control

When people just want to control their pain
Without permission of a contrived system
Established for the privileged to gain
While putting everyone else in prison

Whatever happened to making decisions
Based on consequences
That will affect the children
Seven generations hence?

Franki deMerle

The government is dysfunctional
It dilly dallies around
While its people suffer and die
It doesn't act when solutions are found

Kindness would go a long way
To replace the hard hearted fools
That don't see they make their own demise
Out of selfish tools

They think our country the savior
When it is hated and feared
A self promoted emperor
In fact the world's jester

If only the government were motivated
To actually ease the pain
To realize it's made up of mere people
With kindness to be gained

But ego—the great deluder
Makes fools of us all
Until we learn
We are prisoners all

*

443. for Ray Young Bear

Yes I would accept you
Kayaking on Lost Lake
Up on the side of snowy Hood
Or Horseshoe Bend in view of St Helens

Child of the Universe

I have canoed in Texas
And Tennessee as well
But I prefer the light to slant
Where rainforests still dwell

There is too much directness
In society at large
Too much forcing on us
Opinions that are farce

And when the water freezes
To glide upon a blade
Is to experience freedom
Of the gull, the goose, the jay

But time and climate changes
Those clinging to control
Have brought these dreadful pains
That trouble Nature's soul

And so I would accept you
Gentle soul of peace
Appreciating what is found
In Nature's subtleties

*

444.

Idealists do not survive in business
That requires an artist's job
Successful leaders are not poets

I admire the socialist democracies
The standard of living in Europe
A practical practice of kindness

Franki deMerle

Britain abolished slavery
Through a technicality
And devoted creativity

It takes a tougher skin than mine
To fight and win the battles of time
I am just a poet

I belong in an artistic world
Of music, Nature and literature
I am no political soldier

It's taken me a lifetime
To learn where I am safe
But I have a place

Youth is not a time to know
To learn one's mission
Time is needed to grow

We're guided toward survival
In places that cause harm
Because parents don't trust our karma

Or maybe the lesson for me
Was learning who I am
And where I'm meant to be

And now that's been resolved
I'll move with greater purpose
And confidence involved

Child of the Universe

And maybe my next sojourn
I'll have parents who accept
Me as I am

I must write
I must play music
I must glide across the ice

I must experience beauty
Feel its inherent harmony
For that is kind

*

445.

The epiphany of justice
Is acceptance of oneself
There is no more judgment
Just relief that all is well

*

Franki deMerle

446.

Some look into a well
And see the darkness of despair
I look into the depths
And see life's layers

Spiraling up to present
And on above and beyond
Layer upon layer of feelings
And all that we have done

To live as if this one life
Is all there is to grab
Is to throw away a lifetime
For a moment's stab

To live as if the benefit
Is only found beyond
Is to miss the treasure
We are standing on

There is a bigger picture
Than this one body shows
The epic of the ages
Is here for us to know

*

Child of the Universe

447. for Theodore

I love glitter
I love sparkle
I love iridescence

It's the constant change
That catches the eye
To wonder what is seen

In between the sparkle
In between the glitter
The space between the change

Life is like a flicker
The changing play of light
To write between the lines

*

Franki deMerle

448.

What percentage of the population is homeless?
We know the percentage imprisoned
Less than one percent is aristocrat
How many of the rest of us are left?

This happens over and over again
Humanity recycles
The lessons it fails to learn
Greed versus metaphysical

One can become consumed
With guilt over what is karmic
Or one can become imbued
With cold heartedness

Or one can do what one is able
Enjoy the moment
Learn and hope that the cycle
Is breakable
Wake up and see reality

The undistorted mirror
Particles of light reflecting
Simple human error

Forgive and let it go
We all get tunnel vision
Blindsided by what the unconscious knows
We each live our own mission

So who am I to criticize?
Still I see the madness
I must speak my mind
It's how I'm destined

Child of the Universe

So build the prisons
Raise the walls
The human spirit
Is uncontainable

*

449.

Can you ever just be you
Like a cat does what it needs
Without someone being rude

We always start again
Is there another option—
There always is

A cat will choose to be alone
When annoyed by people
I like staying home

So many beginnings and endings
There is comfort in change
If you don't like what's happening

It's not about likes or dislikes
It's all about satisfaction
Very feline

*

450.

We as mortal beings
Know our bodies die
But there is more to us than that
An eternity of fact

Once removed from bodily life
The life is free to see
Mistakes and missions accomplished
Being in painless freedom

Loves and hates are brought to life
The moment we are born
Into a physical form
A world randomly filled

With some of those we've known
Odds are we will meet and choose
To reenact from how we've grown
Maybe wear each other's shoes

Nothing is ever lost to us
We pick up where we left off
Work through traumas and solve old riddles
Continue or break patterns off

Yes we eventually have our say
We choose who we become
We choose what past we give away
To exposure under the Sun

*

451.

Cuddles for warmth and comfort
Hugs when I come home
I've never been so happy
As when you sucked my nose
Now you're my best buddy
A beautiful lady who knows

Predicting my every move
And reminding me what I've forgotten
No one is more fun to play with
Drinking my decaf green tea
And loving me

Bandit extraordinaire
A cat of exquisite taste
Never late to tea
Don't ever leave me lady
I love you and you know
This is our time

*

Franki deMerle

452.

Some women prefer women
Some prefer men
Some fall in love with their children
But I prefer parakeets and kitty cats
They are my universal companions

Small animals always tell you the truth
They love without condition
And I rearrange my life for them
And love them for their existence
This is happiness

They have their needs
It's my chosen job
To provide for them
As well as cater to their preferences
To make their lives sweet and safe

This is family
This is love
This is honesty
This is trust

*

453.

There's nothing like the fragrance
To touch a feeling ancient
Overpowering the nose
Awakening of a rose

The stillness in one's being
Surrounded by old trees
Calming through the eyes
With commanding height

Nature replaced by cities
Is devolution in extreme
Into overcrowding breakdown
Of civility once found

Community must include
A planet so imbued
With diversity of life
Life means all of life

*

454.

They say depression hurts
This I know is true
Pain that must be covered by lies
I've lied with smiles to hypnotize
My brain into letting loose
The feel good chemicals it deserves
I've lied in search of the truth

Franki deMerle

That suicide is condemned
By men seeking control
Over humanity's feelings
Is lying to say they know
And causes more grief to the suffering
Who mourn what they don't understand
That it was never about them
They were lied to by controlling men
Pretending to have answers
I suppose they should be forgiven
Though forgiveness is not what they chose

I don't trust anyone
Who so easily extinguishes hope
Finding and holding onto it
Is what depression is all about
How easily the dark clouds come
How quickly the fog condenses
It will not disperse upon command
But it can be repressed in some

For a time
By the lie of a smile
Or "I'm fine"
To avoid being treated like a child
Like a criminal who must be chained—
Or is it changed—
Against one's nature

Child of the Universe

I know the darkness
Know it well
Others' crudeness can make it swell
Why can't they just be kind?
That's what churches should ask themselves
Why can't they just be kind?

Life cannot be dictated by rules
Laws are humanly devised
Without an ounce of humane intent
And those who think religion should be strict
Should reconsider being kind

I know the storm that comes inside
Is chemical
I know in society it's required to lie
To hide the truth
Hope can be obliterated
By disrespect and antiquated
Ignorance learned by rote
Hope can be annihilated
By those who talk too much
When all they should do is be kind

I know how cruel the lack of hope
That can't be cured by prayer
It can be faced by knowing it
When neurons fail to fire
The signal light that lifts the dark
How to do it is what's hard
And if darkness sets in long enough
Life might as well be done

Franki deMerle

Depression is like drowning
Ridicule is not rope
Condemnation is concrete affixed
Ignorance sinks the lifeboat
So I smile to remind me I might as well laugh
When I desperately need to cry
Sometimes all I have is my lie

I lived so long in an alien world
Confused by trying to fit in
For only so long one can pretend
Before the cracks set in
And all those who were so cruel—
So smug and so self assured—
They would protect their own
By breaking their own rules
But I was never one of them
A fact made clear every day
And shoved in my face
While I did my best to smile
Would it have hurt them to be kind?

Child of the Universe

Never again will I dare to live
Among those trained to kill
Who hold themselves above the law
Above humanity
Above me
Who mock those they are meant to shield
And convolute the term "to serve"
Then serve themselves and steal
From those they were meant to defend
Openly professing how much they detest
Those they were meant to protect
Those who truly deserve respect
Those who try to be kind

And what of all the suicides?
They did the best they could
There is no sin requires forgiveness
Except for those who judge

*

455.

Small animals don't need our lifespan
To understand the world
They don't waste time on addictions
And farce the way we do

They understand what's necessary
The things that mean the most
They understand our feelings
And show us sensitivity

How can they not be loved
For all they share and give
If not for my small companions
I'd have little reason to live

Their lessons carry over
To the people in my life
How to empathize and be honest
In the midst of pain and strife

So much nonsense interferes
So much garbage clutters our minds
Having small companions
Is a constant reminder to be kind

*

456.

Miss you little lady bug
Underweight and desperate for love
Snuggled up against my neck when I first picked you up

Child of the Universe

Ever so special when you slept in my bed
Time and illness had taken their toll
Though not your spirit
Ever cradled in my arms

You were special
Always will be to me
You are true love

May the Universe be kind to you
As you were to me
May we find each other again
And be together eternally

*

457.

We have a global society
No longer in harmony
With our very own livelihood

This makes no sense on any level
When imbalanced leaves us so disheveled
Something has to give

I go into my meditation
Feel safe within my sphere of protection
I know it isn't so

I reach out to my one connection
Silver angel voice of heaven
And plead my cause—he knows

I know we're not meant to meet
In this life til all is complete
And the past is leveled

Franki deMerle

But there will be another time
When iridescent colors shine
And peace is our priority
Again?

This is a violent planet
And this country's history of greed
Can't justify all the killing
So look to needs

People need their dreams
They need camaraderie
They meet on common ground

If governments just take care of needs
Of the people
There is harmony

Home of the brave and free translates
To home of the rich and greed
And homeless

Elizabeth the first would imprison them
Traveling minstrels as vagabonds
History lies to us all

She murdered her cousin
For not murdering their cousin
Covered up all
But that's the way it's always been
Carpenter royally destined
Crucified

He knew to take care of people's needs
He knew not to rule for rich and greed
He died

Child of the Universe

It's ok cause they made him a god
Pretended he came back to life
Maybe in a different time

But the god thing covered up
What he was really about
And so it goes

Go back as far as you like
Peaceful societies are scandalized
By the demons

I live in a demon country
Governed by rich and greed
Demonizing peace

Even science fiction knows
You must take care of needs
But it's just in shows

When we meet it won't be here
In a country based on fear
We'll be free to speak

Meanwhile I have my sphere of protection
Where you can join my meditation
Anytime

*

458.

Light comes down at all angles
We see accordingly
Wind blows in all directions
And we all breathe

Throughout life is similarity
All perceived differently
Joy is in discovering
Another perspective

How sad for those suffering
Defects of personality
That cause them to see the beauty
As defective

For this there are wars and slavery
For this there is no diplomacy
Once the sick are able to convince
Politicians to fear diversity

Light still shines at all angles
Wind still blows the dust of all
Water flows down regardless of what
The blind and deaf fear will fall

Those truly blind see more
Those truly deaf hear the wind
Joy is found in differences
Each day we begin again

Pity the souls who cannot determine
Fact from self opinion
For they are the disabled requiring assistance
It's a contagious human condition

Child of the Universe

When intellect replaced instinct
Ego-based opinion led the way
We are still capable of the intuitive
But we must listen instead of praying

To the wind and the water that falls all around
And learn to keep an ear to the ground
For the planet supports all but does not judge
A species flying faster than sound

Bringing change faster and faster for the sake of itself
Without contemplating the nature of wealth
Found in four legged angels and flight paths of the wild
Their habitats and our very own language of smiles

Facts are not the whole of truth
Statistics are manmade
Understanding Nature requires
Feeling the change of light each day

*

459.

In every church
There is a dictator
Demanding control
And those willing
To blindly follow

In every place
Is a crocodile
With weakness and fear as prey
Thick skinned
Its blood runs cold

Empathy is interspatial
Force is its murderer
Killing ways of life
The natural way of life
Of Nature's children

In every family
There is misunderstanding
And a need to accept and let go

*

Child of the Universe

460.

OK, I mix my pronouns up
But it's a tongue too beautiful not to try
My vocabulary is handicapped
By a country culturally biased

En boca cerrada no entran moscas
Escrito en mi propio riesgo
En mi defensa
El lápiz es supuestamente de una mordida

Los extremistas deben tener las traducciones
Arrogancia no le gusta pensar
En las capas de la percepción
Disculpen los deslices

De mis esfuerzos
Ya que se esfuerzan por encontrar mi ritmo
Y tratar de alguna manera la rima
En capas de idioma

Una vez pensé
Como busco mi ritmo
Se lo aprendo

A closed mouth lets no bugs in
I write at my own risk
In my defense
The pen is mightier than a sting

Extremists must have translations
Arrogance doesn't like to think
In layers of perception
So please excuse the awkwardness

Franki deMerle

Of my efforts
As I strive to find my rhythm
And somehow seek the rhyme
In layers of language

I mistakenly thought in my youth
That time would enlighten
We would move forward
And learn tolerance

But now I know
Nothing is certain
When it comes to humans
They don't always grow

And so I offer
My humble thoughts
As a simple
Example

I want to scream
Learn
Look it up
Value education

Using the brain
Feels good
There is pain and hard work
That brings love

Espérame
I will learn
Learn with me
We'll have fun

Child of the Universe

The sun rises
The darkness fades
Communication
Reveals the way

*

461.

No harm, no foul, no longer computes
In the insane world of sensationalist fools
Who would imprison honest beings
For wanting to be together

Airport security is the joke of the century
So many people afraid to die
News flash—we will anyway
Death is regulated only by time

People demand security
Because they are insecure
It doesn't exist in corporeal life
Why must the reality of death be denied?

Could it be they don't want to reap the effects
Of not being willing to share?
The law of possession is itself a lie
We have only for what we care

Fear of death is the product of a false, jealous god
Who would condemn his own children to hell
A good mother nurtures her children until well
We can choose, we can choose, we can choose what we will

Franki deMerle

No system that works is ever secure
Security full force stops all
Justice is a balancing act
Or there is no justice at all

Instead of justice we get vengeance
"'Vengeance is mine,' sayeth the Lord"
Prosecutors and legislators playing God
Wreak havoc on everyone

It's now a crime to make a mistake
I've never met a perfect human being
But fear brings out the judge in everyone
Blind justice—no one is seeing

How we've ridiculed what once was democracy
Because we got scared of reality
We act like bullies to the rest of the world
And they expose us as silly

When you run at a pace with no time to think
You're not going to function at your best
What sense does it make to fear your own death?
Slow down for a dignified breath

What funny creatures we are who sell
The time of our lives so we can live well
There is no comfort in security
And no security is comfortable

Why pay the airlines to submit to their control
And sacrifice dignity
Why bother to go anywhere at all
When you are where you need to be

Child of the Universe

Grand destinations are just advertisements
To get your money while causing you stress
If you need an escape you have your dreams
Vacation at home is the best
We don't need crap we're told we need
Common sense has been lost in the fray
Consumer debt has passed rationality
Replaced by material greed

How much is too much?
You know deep inside
Is addiction your purpose
Or are you just along for the ride?

Does your inner worth guide you to dignity
Or will you strip for security
That won't prevent your corporeal demise
Do you value true freedom?

Do other people tell you when you are free
To meet with friends you want to see?
Do you recognize when you hand over control
Of your life to another party?

I've been there and it's easy to not see
How silently we give away our liberty
And let others tell us what to believe
Because we want to trust and be able to believe

It's harder to take back individual control
To choose not to engage with human animals
To choose not to sink to a primal level of fear
To be free in the moment of what's really here

Franki deMerle

This is the information age
So why are so many uninformed
Of the myriad of alternate perspectives
Available if they can afford
A library card

Turn off the chatter of stupid broadcasts
Saying to panic over terrorists
Within the inner sea of your soul
All is calm

Senseless beauty shared for free
Does more to contribute to global peace
Than any presence of military
When people take time to think

Random kindness in advance
Is worth more than a political promise
I'll choose what I believe
And set my own self free

*

Child of the Universe

462. for LVH

It's difficult to shed the shackles
That bound one in the past
The pain of limitations

Compares not to the work to be done
To overcome the habit
Of finding comfort in the handicap

Disabilities not faced are daily difficulties
But having to see what determined their being
Is extraordinary

And then begins the painful journey
El premier paso es el más difícil
Yo también—I struggle daily

But what we create is beautiful
The hope of surpassing pain
Compassion—que maravilla

We see others struggling and comprehend
The hardest work is done within
Quietly we reach around the world
And hold hands

*

463.

Accelerate
All becomes a blur
But the feeling inside
Addictive sensation
Works for me
The sudden release
Dropping, floating
Falling freely
Much like flying
In my dreams

*

464.

A poet may be an idealist or cynic
But thoughts must be expressed
Simplicity reduced to childlike rhyme
Or complexity employed in the text

I've broken all the rules
After all they were only tools
Irregular rhythms and imperfect rhymes
Invisible punctuation
But the verses are mine

Mixed metaphors can deepen symbolism
The readers take away only what they comprehend
But the unconscious that interprets information
From this Universe finds its vents

Child of the Universe

Like volcanic ranges releasing their steam
The meaning is in the mist
The lava of verse flows into the stream
Of human consciousness presumably civilized
And waits on its page to be recognized

All is cyclical—this too is a cycle
To die and to return
How we live our lives is personal
Infinite capacity to learn

Forgiveness frees from pain
Kindness lights the day
Compassion supersedes our species
It is the only sensible way

Beyond that all is superfluous
Chatter to pass the time
So quickly slides into judgmental gossip
And someone is maligned

We do enough of that to ourselves
So much cruelty comes from pain
And forgiveness is on the medicine shelf
We just have to reach for and take

Many choose the academic way
I prefer Nature and life
But the point is to learn how to survive
Without becoming unkind

Franki deMerle

We've carried the answers for centuries
In history and inside
The reason prayers don't get answered
Is because to listen you must be quiet

They don't come from mystical gurus
Though they may have understood
But inevitably someone perverts the message
And makes profit instead of good

And that's not condemnable
Human vice is part of us all
Which is why we have the ultimate power
To forgive

It's throughout the living kingdom
Though masked by the will to live
We're all one ecosystem
Bodies with egos that forget

The lava vents and steam pours forth
Like creation upon a page
The same old cycle of events
Full of beauty, wonder and rage

Mirrors are for forgiving
And appreciating the beauty revealed
This is the path of kindness
And the only way to be healed

Religion is not needed
Just two or four feet on the ground
There's no need for a leader
When the path has already been found

Child of the Universe

A woman doesn't need a husband
A man doesn't need a wife
We have everything that is needed
We have life

I'm just another poet
Spewing words upon the page
That rise from collective unconscious
In the information age

Death is part of the cycle
I know my turn will come
But I've been there and I remember
It's traumatic but it's part of the fun

The mirror will tell you your true face
The mirror reveals how you reached this place
I'm facing the same in my life
The choices were all mine

May we be happy
May we be peaceful
May we not suffer
May we be kind

Anger over the many lies
Is natural but hurts only you
Humiliating to admit you believed
What you later learned not to be true

Natural to experience emotions
Toward those that caused abuse
But only helpful if the knowledge
Leads you to the truth

Pity the soul who cannot feel
Pity the damaged one trapped in a tunnel
Pity those who mock others
Who wear feelings on a sleeve
They are afraid of both dying and living

Every wound sensitizes
And teaches how to empathize
That is the source of kindness
And the only hope of life

*

465.

Every day we're given chances to be kind
How many have I let slip away?
Doesn't matter now because more will come my way

Each person trapped in a body
In their own individual hell
We can wait for change
Or we can change
This present moment is eternal

*

Child of the Universe

466. from a dream

People play games and box me in
They don't understand I can't do this again
Selfishness and politics
Don't understand I'm ready to quit

I felt trapped in some kind of hell
Tried escape to no avail
Until an angel in my unconscious
Caught me when I fell

I prefer the style of the cat
You are more the dog
No reason why we can't get along

You need your audience
And I need to be heard
Friendship does not preclude each the other
But must be equal terms

Is there trust?
Is there love?
Is it superficial?

You came to me and made promises
That must be kept or be lies
Remember how I comforted you?
But we must equalize

I'll see you again soon enough
If you lie I'll call you on it
Memory is not obsession

Franki deMerle

Amazing it takes centuries
For one to realize
That ego, desires and duties
Only result in lies

Caring is not out of style
Nor immature to crave an impression
That you remember our fall

I was naïve in belief
For you I cannot speak
That those I trusted deceived
I sincerely had no idea

But if you must control me
Go away and leave me alone
Because I must be free

Yet you had bloody hands
That I washed for you
And I still don't understand
What is left for me to do

Next time we meet I ask you
Let's start over
And just accept each other

I know we must repeat
What we started long ago
We eventually will meet
And that is all I know

Do you hold some grudge
Or feel superior to me?
All I ask is a gentle touch
And recognition of equality

Child of the Universe

Thrice now you have left me
In tears as though a child
I'm due for you to comfort me
And respect my casual style

I represent no country
No church nor cultural mores
I am who I am just simply
And I deserve to be heard

*

467.

So much a soul can understand
Sometimes I just do not
But when I look down deep inside
The dreaded doings were alive
Where I forgot

Power corrupts and creates the desire
To make others do one's bidding
The very notion is silly
Sends hate and disillusionment
In combination an all consuming fire

The notion of one person over another
A hierarchical formula
For disaster
This world will have its way
Of destruction

What of the beauty and gentleness?
Does it not belong here?
Must it be brushed by so quickly
And eliminated so easily
In the power struggles?

Franki deMerle

If we only paid attention
But oh how the mind can wander
If we only listened to our hearts
So much would be different—so much kinder
So much would not fall apart

But we are who we are
It is what it is
We learn best we can
We suffer
Until we live and let live

Meanwhile I hide in my corner
Safe with the best of my life
And try to protect my perimeter
While staying out of sight
Doing my best to change inside

And so it goes
No one cares what a poet knows
Or doesn't
Seven billion all alone
With kindness

The myth of the animal kingdom
There is much kindness there
The ability to care and share
We have intellectualized away
To appear in control

*

Child of the Universe

468. for Thomas Fallis

Kind assistance
Offered with patience
And a smile
Gives so much warmth
To this troubled world
Like a candle shining light
For a while

When I touched your cold hand
I could feel you smile
Down at me
When I see you again
It will be my privilege
When we meet

*

469.

The airwaves are full of betrayal
Every dog has its day
Each soul takes its turn in the spotlight
Then moves to the shadows to wait

Waiting and wondering like everyone else
Why do the "leaders" betray us?
Everyone is waiting
Waiting for forgiveness

*

470. for Steve Matous

Hope you're well—I am
You saved me so much grief
By exploring and explaining

Living is so much simpler
When we know what we're dealing with
Understanding cannot be overrated
It's all we have to work with

*

471.

Country of value to the world
Hot and cold extremes
Inventive people
Living there
Exceptionally

*

Child of the Universe

472.

Play your guitars my friends
Our time here will come to an end
Don't let success go to your head
All you wanted was recognition

I've been singing along in seclusion
Billions of voices raised in song
That don't care at all
Who has the microphone

In countries with social democracy
Folk movements aren't repressed like here at home
This country governed by monopolies
Thinks music can be replaced by greed

But voices are singing about the truth
People are singing about being human
Peasants know what life is all about
To work, live simply, and sing out loud

It's never too late to change your tune
And give up the struggle for power
There is no controlling the Universe
So we sing of the wisdom to cower

We sing of the courage not to kill
And the safety humility brings
So many hear and never listen
They can't learn if they don't question anything

Beauty is the flower of honesty
Its strength is its integrity
Folk music sings and the people speak
The meaning of their priorities

Franki deMerle

Play your guitars my friends
Sing out loud and strong
Tell it like it is
The greedy elite don't belong

In this earthly wonderland
Of ever changing beauty
And opportunities
For kindness

The government is out of control
Its spinning has made "leaders" dizzy
They've lost their way and their balance
Because they're not listening

Folk music sings about beauty
And truth in simplicity
People don't want more prisons
They just want homes, jobs, and peace

So play your guitars my friends
And sing in every language
Sing the songs that teach
Those despairing to sing

*

473.

I spent a career serving a country
Hell bent on raising hell
I thought I might have a positive influence
I failed

Child of the Universe

War is a culture for dysfunctionals
Who trust others to tell them their purpose
Like following a false messiah
To one's destruction

Military have done many good deeds
Many honorable souls sincerely striving to serve
But political leadership pollutes the process
And good becomes soaked with blood

Each attempts to do a duty
But power corrupts with control
Of innocent lives who follow willingly
Fulfilling the corporate call

It's all about the money
It all comes down to greed
Those that choose to play the game
Do it for their own "needs"

Not recognizing the difference
Wants become greed becomes "needs"
Not knowing when to stop
Or to start turning

And others be damned to poverty
In those other countries
So we can say we've won
Lives are not saved by guns

May I never again be bewitched
By political advertisements
And promises of noble causes
Involving death and destruction

Franki deMerle

May I maintain a healthy distance
From those offering false assistance
Weapons for money
Monetary democracy

The only answers lie in kindness
A true path practices nonviolence
Builds on integrity
Live and let be

Let this be the human legacy
Let this define our humanity
To not try to control with lies
To simply be honest and kind

*

474. for Brother Cornel West

You maintain perspective and speak the truth
Your words lighten my heart and give me hope
When hateful things darken my mood
That one who cares and speaks out is good

There is such depth to be found in kindness
For strangers, for family, for corporate lawyers
You have remembered the suffering ones
And remind us not to forget

A dream must find realization
It must find a plan and a path
Takes hard work and frustration
Takes being straight with the facts

Child of the Universe

That dream of justice for all
That we share is a work in progress
But it's one we can't allow to fail
For the simple sake of kindness

So please keep on speaking
We are listening
To your inspiration
To the truth of your love

*

475

Letting go of what brings stress
These things that are least important
Learning is a lifelong process

My nervous system screams in pain
A definite form of awakening
To the aftereffects of being chained

But I am glad to let it go
Not what I want to take from here
All things are remembered in the soul
Until you bless them and leave them here

Such opportunity memory gives
To choose what choices to shed
The continuity of why we live
With baggage carried over from death

It is hard for us who cling
To precious emotions and memories
Who fear to part with anything

Franki deMerle

Amassing is not who I am
It covers up the truth
I must let go to find my path

And yet I carry no regrets
It happened, it was, and it's done
Knowing is a source of rest
Let go and I am not gone

In this life I've lived many times
Had many friends, jobs and homes
Made broken hearts into wind chimes
Gained all by letting it go

*

476.

We come to Earth
To lose our pride
We are born to learn
To compromise
But not with those who hate
It's up to them to change their ways
We can only teach what we know
By showing through example
For that we must be mindful
Of ourselves
This is how to change the world
There is no other way
One must be mindful of oneself
And not engage in hate
Positions of esteem are not needed
Examples of the lowliest are heeded
When they shame those who know better
Each of us has equal chance
To leave this world enhanced

*

Franki deMerle

477. for Lewis Black

What would Nature do for laughs
If there were no people?
Well, yes there are cats
I know that birds laugh

I love your Hysterium
I want to be part
A noble endeavor
Laughter's good for the heart

Whoever created
This vast Universe
Didn't mess with conformity
But loved the diverse

No wiser words have been spoken
To heal everything we have broken
By seeking the Holy Joke

*

Child of the Universe

478.

The young have no concept of consequence
So much is public now
They lack the privacy in which to learn—
In which to make their mistakes

A child should not have to explain
What he does not understand
Punishment should not be so harsh
When correction just needs explanation

Some occurrences should be off limits
To the press and the police
Humiliation becomes degradation
And leads to no self-esteem

This is not justice
It is not rehabilitation
To ruin a life that's only begun
By blind condemnation

For a society that worships youth
We don't respect our young
Enough to take the time to share
That actions cannot be undone

*

Franki deMerle

479. for BJ

Little sister, the world can be cruel
To those who are kind
You are like a butterfly
Able to adapt
And withdraw when it is time
Only to come back with beautiful wings
To drink the nectar of beautiful things
You've been the crawling caterpillar
Now emerging in true form
Your true calling is in the midst of art
And colorful beautiful forms

*

Child of the Universe

480.

Is one in need required
To subscribe to your beliefs
Before you can see
We're all people?

I dream someday of a country
Where each voice is equally heard
Instead of this divided nation
Of meaningless anger

We're not meant to be an empire
We're not meant to conquer others
We should first look to our own conduct
And how we treat each other

Surely we can think beyond all this
Us versus them
I dream someday we'll seize ourselves
And wake up

So here we are in stasis
Repeating lessons not learned
I yearn for an oasis
Where all individuals have worth

*

481.

An individual snowflake
Falls wondrously unique
And blends with other snowflakes
To make a blanket complete
And then comes warmth and melting away
Once unique now gone
Then someday reforms

Franki deMerle

We go to sleep at night
Neither body nor mind has died
Both are active but out of sight
They reunite in daylight
Refreshed and better informed
Enlightened by insight
Revived

The tide flows in and out
In between are footprints on the beach
They come and go with the ebb and flow
Rarely are they seen
But I remember the sand between my toes
Even if no one else knows
I remember

We breathe in and out
The proof of being alive
The body breaks or wears out
The body is not the life
The energy goes out
Not destroyed but energized
Life

Daylight fades to night
The sun has not died
Only the day has slipped away
Beyond our sight
Nighttime wakes to daybreak
Return of what seemed lost
We live again

Child of the Universe

We are but one expression
Of all that is
The natural cycle of continuation
Repetition for what's unlearned
Learning that brings evolution
Understanding of what is
And appreciation

There is no chosen people
There is no superior race
There is no higher life form
We all share equal space
All deserve respect
And consideration for we are one
Universe

*

482.

We need food, water and shelter
We need to care for each other
We need to learn to use our bodies
And our brains

We need to feel fulfillment
We need to feel useful
We need to grow in understanding
We need meaning

There is beauty to be found
In places and things such as these
Lest we forget the life worth living
Is full of beauty

Franki deMerle

When did we begin to believe
In advertising?
Again it is the need for beauty
We need to believe

People fall into consumer black holes
Until debt leaves them no owned things
But if they've grown in understanding
They find meaning

*

483.

The scribe is but a messenger
The bearer of meaningful thought
The messages are sometimes hard to bear
And leave the scribe distraught
Over details of communicating
Without getting it all wrong
Losing sight of the bigger picture
And the beauty of the song

The scribe no less imperfect
Than surprised recipient
Cannot deal with questions
Like where should we begin
Or how is it that this is
The messenger delivers
And of necessity moves on

*

484.

The world is imperfect
Get over it
Whatever happens
We share it

My mother raised me
In the art of complaining
I was good at it
It left me with depression
And stress

We are at our best
During acts of kindness

*

485.

Existence is
The moment expands
Beyond boundaries
When definitions cease
There is no you and me
The colors blend softly
We the world gently
Embrace ourself

The concept of enemy
Is a fabrication
For which there is
No lasting justification
Just people holding onto pain
Defining differences leads to hate
Until you see the Universe
As a place of diverse beauty
Joyous sounds are loud

And there is peace in silence
We are not in stasis
We either decay or grow
And the sound of a moan
Evokes the need to comfort
For pain is an opportunity
To share living contact

*

486.

The body breaks
We find another
Life and death
Become each other

*

Child of the Universe

487.

What good is education not applied?
What use is knowing what you like
If you let your likes be brushed aside?
What purpose is served by remembering the past
If you don't learn by what's been tried?

What is the point of pain
If sensation does not train
The mind to listen to its body?
Why have a body and a mind
If they don't communicate?

The senses of the body
Are doors and windows to outside
If we don't observe what we perceive
Is the body really alive?

If the lesson is forgiveness
And the practice is compassion
And our motives are other than kindness
Can happiness ever find us?

*

Franki deMerle

488.

The flutter of so many heartbeats
Working to pump the air
To the point of physical exhaustion

Move quickly
Time flies as a blur
Of beauty and exertion

Oh, the taste is sweet
The nectar of eternity
Must be suckled constantly

Never mind what trials there be
Focus on the beauty
That tastes so sweet

*

Child of the Universe

489. for Bob

The flower sheds its seeds to the wind
There is no endeavor to control
It accepts that they will be its children
Who they are it does not know

A good parent assists a child to become
Whoever that child really is
Without attempt to dominate or control
And finds joy in whatever is

Domination stifles and harms
Holds back the soul to be known
Irreparable damage can be done by control
Faith always trusts and lets go

Joy is found in appreciation
Of the flower newly bloomed
The color, the shape, the ever sweet fragrance
That joy reveals the soul's truth

While one's own life may be cultivated
In whatever manner one may choose
The delicate seeds must be released
For wind's spirit alone to guide youth

Who will always have their own dreams and talents
To light their journey's path
For only their souls will know their true purpose
It's up to them to do the math

The seeds will find where best they grow
Some admired, some die unappreciated
But the cycle of life will not be controlled
Regardless how it's interpreted

Franki deMerle

Our job is to appreciate
Our joy is to fall in love
With the beings we meet along the way
And let go when the time comes

*

490.

Some are born with prejudice
Some are born with preferences
Some come to see what will be
It's easier if you know yourself
And can see you as others see

Denial gives us blind spots
These are lessons that must be learned
Best to explore oneself carefully
Than to risk being burned
This is a lesson I've learned

It can hurt to try new things
When inside a voice is saying
You're headed into a lifetime of darkness
I could have found another way
But then no one gets out unscathed

This life is a school for slow learners
It's really a hell of a place
The trick is to learn as much as you can
Before the final graduation—
To try to understand the system

Which is that it isn't about us
It isn't about us at all
It's patterns and trends and balance
That affect us all
That we affect through kindness

Child of the Universe

Because it's not about us
This pain we cause ourselves
It's the bigger picture
That governs where each one fell
The system is universal

Focus on the petty details
Lost in hate or thought
And be a pawn of greater forces
Or realize the cosmos
Is really what we're part of

*

491.

The verses rise up from inside
They do not let me sleep
I close my eyes and I must write

This broken body needs its rest
The mind will not be still
Until it has expressed
All that it will

The living must have sleep
Dive deep
The mind comes up for air
Comes up to share

*

492.

At most times it appears to me
That each thinks
Things should or not be
Acceptance of the moment is one thing

But rejection of improvement is foolish
Humans are so afraid of change
Security does not come from repetition—
That's boredom

*

493.

So many archetypes
We choose from Nature's finest
But the greatest symbol
Of all of civilization
Is the wheel

Its movement, its mandala
The gears that work machines
The charts on which we plot the stars
The essential truth of our being

Is a circle going around
Enabling our travel
A journey that abounds
In stories of itself

Some true—some not so much
The symbol of humanity
It is us

*

Child of the Universe

494.

Young inquiring minds
Determined to save lives
Become overwhelmed with information
And give in from exhaustion and confusion
To diagnose by health insurance equations

Who knew?
Growing pains they told me
Of course I was depressed
There was no release from pain
Undiagnosed distress

Many doctors come from outside the US
God bless them for putting up with our mess
But who knew it would come to this?
Pain from a life ended badly
Following till it could be mended

We can't deal with the pain of death at the time
Once it's done it must wait until we're alive
And recognize what needs to be resolved
How can it be diagnosed without memory?

I have reclaimed my life
I understand so much more—so much gained
I've learned empathy for others in pain
I have possibilities to entertain

I can be well again
Someday the pain will be gone
But why can't a cure for greed be found?

*

495.

Sweetness of smell and taste
Is not appreciated in haste
Making haste complicates
Pause is needed to ruminate
Listening requires attention to space
Instead of society's busy pace
Connecting with moments of the day
Inner voices are able to have their say
To allow the silence of relaxation
Youthfulness needs for restoration

*

496.

Rhythm is the heartbeat
Rhyme is the song of the mind
The soul of the poet is compelled to speak
In patterns that intertwine

Thought long ago forgotten
Ideas that seem to make sense
Society has stepped from metaphor
To virtual lack of depth

Busy always and never still
Noise and commotion bombard
To listen to silence is like writing with a quill
Today's toys annoy a true bard

For the rhythm of life moves slowly
Not at this frantic pace
No time is spent exploring
The meanings in the lines of a face

Child of the Universe

Or are the young souls of this world
Here only for physical sensation?
How quickly that pursuit curdles
Into meaningful starvation

The pendulum swings each way in time
The outward tide turns and returns
Someone hears the song of another's mind
And thoughts from the silence are learned

*

497.

People with a scapegoat
Are not mature adults
They ramble on about the faults
And end up sounding dumb
When the evidence reveals
The fault is theirs

We all do it sometimes
We all want to stay young
But self-denial projects itself
Outward away from what
We don't want to be
But we are—we just don't see

When the issue is not about us
We make it us and them
And distract others from the truth
Of what we could get done
If only we weren't so stubborn
And could see past our illusion

*

Franki deMerle

498.

Darkness is a comfort
A place where peace prevails
Where man-made lights do not intrude
To break the quiet spell

The creatures of the night
Have specialized in stealth
And protect the quiet
So needed for good health

It is like a security blanket
That falls upon the ground
Where all who seek the quiet
May move within its bounds

*

499. for Richard Eberhart

You met your mark
You caught your prey
We are all deluded
By time and space

I felt your touch
So gentle and true
Somewhere in time
I must know you

You have my heart
You know my soul
We are not apart
But part of the whole

*

Child of the Universe

500.

How we work with words inside us
Expresses all around us
I fear I've done much damage to myself
Clichés, quotes and recordings
The brain must work in concert
I have not been forgiving—truth to tell

Holding onto feelings deeply
The brain takes everything literally
And reveals it in my suffering
From being overly critical
Of all that I have written down
But editing must be done

To me words are important
But they too change with time
As languages evolve
To render me but a moment
That others quickly forget
While I too have moved on

*

501.

The world is having a conversation
With itself
Blogs and internet communications
Thought wealth

The barriers of privacy
Come down
And all are seen
Truth found

*

502.

Pain expresses displeasure
And vents in trifles
That change to humor

*

503.

What is literal, what is metaphor
Is for the reader to choose
If I can conjure past and future
The both are mine to use

Time is all around us
In memories, thoughts and dreams
I can be child and elderly
Reversed or in between

And I can tell a story
With characters all but me
Or I can choose to look inside
And see all people equally

*

Child of the Universe

504.

The soldier is confident
He has liberated the oppressed
Who are forced to welcome the armed
The working people who have no other choice
But to cater to egos to survive

The soldier projects himself
Onto his enemy
Any guilt he carries
Any harm done inadvertently
Becomes that of the enemy

To be able to learn how to kill
The soldier must truly believe
The perception others drill
Into his very being
He dares not question authority

This is a choice we all must make
Will we question or follow blindly?
Will we remain open to what our senses say
Or relinquish free will randomly?
Will we allow ourselves to project a movie
Or live each moment consciously?

*

505.

My body is aging and in pain
But I'm having the time of my life
Now is the moment of realization
Now is the production of my creation

Nature experiences spontaneity
Every day, every season
What has taken me so long to awaken
To my own being?

*

506.

Pull out the scar tissue
Like the roots of a weed
Left growing too long
Deep and strong
No more needed

Inhibiting fresh healthy growth
Strangling freedom
Must be removed
For new seeds to be planted
With room for their roots

Something fresh and beautiful
Whose time is arriving
Life that is bountiful
A body surviving
A time of pain is passed

*

Child of the Universe

507.

A baby doesn't feel for others
It knows only its own needs
Nor has it ability to judge correctly
Those from which it feeds

But when a child does not mature
Grows only in its body
It judges everyone around
Incompliant with personal greed

Many adults aren't mature beings
They're just grown babies suckling
And cannot determine what's best for any
Much less family or country

I live in a divided country
Of those seeking the ideal
And of those damaged babes
Who are afraid to feel

*

508.

When you leave you don't take your things
Not your home, your food or your earnings
You only take what you've learned

*

509.

I feel things deeply
Others are surprised
I tell the truth
When expected to lie

But we all lie sometimes
And everyone gets hurt
When I write it isn't me
It's the universe

The stars that made us
Still shine bright
Though far away and long gone
Still share their light

We are like them
If we choose to be
And so my mere words
From the universe speak

*

510. for PTE

Woman on a power trip
Causing pain for others
How can she do it?

Do they not suffer
In her imagination?
Doesn't she have a mirror?

*

Child of the Universe

511. for Victoria

You offered me friendship
Only you didn't mean it
I don't understand
What is it you wanted?

A list of acquaintances?
"Call when you need me"
But you were never there
Never answered your messages

You're such a nice person
Why wall yourself off
With someone else's rules?
I don't understand

But you have your own world
And I hope you're safe there
Just don't invite others
Unless you really care

*

512.

I don't care for society's dictates
I don't care for business insensitivity
I compare myself to no one
And avoid competitive insecurity

The world, the universe, life, the One
Is gentle, kind, forgiving
In my experience religious extremes
Are the only ones who judge harshly

Woman is free again
She has been liberated
She will not willingly be re-enslaved
She will not be berated

She is the voice of reason
When emotion is misunderstood
She is the mother of the species
That no longer requires manhood

So let go of entitlement
I will not clean or cook for you
I have missions of my own
I'll not be judged by you

*

513.

When does it stop
This runaway train
Of emotions, opinions, ideas?
When does it rest?
When it runs out of fuel?
Interrupted gets thrown off the track
It's up to the engineer
Maintenance and precaution
A choice of destination
Not where but when
Alternative transportation
Stillness, calm within

*

Franki deMerle

514.

The brain is imaginative
It filters perception
By how we program it
It follows instructions

It provides what we need
Real or not
We delve in or step back
And look at what we've wrought

I needed to feel loved
I reached out
In the safety of dreams
And he's real

But we live differently
So I'll wait
Another life maybe
Or in between space

But he was there
He responded
He pulled me up
He cared

So I'll not bother him
But consider his space
In his waking hours
I have no place

So dreams are real
And awake an illusion
Or both are the same
Inverted intrusion

Child of the Universe

Cerebral spinal fluid
Is the ocean of emotion
Entered and left through breath
Pure vibration

The body's a frame
The brain is the engine
But love and emotion
Open doors for transition

*

515.

First people fought for the right to life and liberty
Now they fight for death with dignity
And rightly so
But being unsatisfied is a state of mind
That can become a way of life
Or can lead to helping others
However temporary
What they really want to know
Is how to cope with pain
A sensation
Don't judge it
Easy to say
It doesn't go away
But it helps to accept it

*

Franki deMerle

516. for Dr. Tom Dooley

Trauma is invisible
To the naked eye
The burning fire sizzled
You reached inside
And with a feather
Waved good-bye

It's all in the past
I hear you say
Your voice is with me
Every day

The key of release
From so much pain
That's all in the past
And fading away

*

517.

Tunnel vision seems to be the default position
I'm trying to see the big picture
I've always been good at the details
But the inner voice commands listening

Pain is a signal same as joy
They share the same neuroreceptor
Turn the page and go beyond
We are so much more than what's here on Earth

Child of the Universe

Worlds collide—is that not painful?
But so beautiful to see
The gases glowing out in space
Way beyond the miniscule "me"

I write because it is what I do
Not because I am unique
For me it is healing therapy
I write because I think

Someday I will mature
I will see the big picture
Someday I will learn to converse
As a child of the Universe

*

518. for Adrian

I'm so grateful you survived the camps
To help me verify my past
I needed validation

So many you have helped this way
I would not have guessed the obvious
Similarities of face

I comprehended patterns
I understood the dreams
Held onto memories

But you've verified scientifically
What I could not
And done so for so many

In a world polluted with conventions
That are only human inventions
The truth means so much

We don't know where we'll be next time
Best not to make enemies or take a side
But to all be kind

*

519.

This world is such a violent place
It's easy to succumb to fear
Many try to protect themselves
By controlling others with power

Child of the Universe

This world can be a painful place
Some retreat inside a cocoon
In peace and contemplation
They grow until they bloom

Tanta belleza en el mundo
How others can be so blind
I do not know
Pero le dolió mi corazón

Aloha noka oe
I wish you all the best
Until the next my friends
Mahalo, multsu mesc

*

520.

The Universe bestows its gifts
Each individual receives a unique
Spectrum of light with which to shine

Sometimes buried underneath emotions
Or traumas or passing of time
But always ready to shine

To claim it is to negate it
It belongs to the Universe
Never mine

Gratitude is all the thanks required
Set reactions aside
And reveal the Light

*

521.

Ici je suis
Ich bin hier
Soy aquí
I am here
Where else would I be?

*

522. for Kathy L

May your cats only go in the box
May your dogs bring in only mud
May coyotes stay far from your door
And may your days be filled with sun

May climate change only warm your heart
May songbirds cheer you up
May you always take time for art
When you've got a minute, ring me up

*

523.

The molecules form a body
Breath enters and brings it to life
No one in Nature gives a damn
That another's feelings are true and tried

The human world destroys other species
Squashes hopes and devours cherished dreams
Like a black hole full of misery
Mocking sensitivity

Child of the Universe

Perception of a better way
If expressed will be punished
Expression of an honest life
If detected will be smashed

We hold to the delusion
There's a great, wise, karmic plan
When truth is just confusion
That no one understands

Life is fiction like a dream
Reality disguised
No matter how much we cry and scream
We simply suffer and die

Oh joy, we get to do it again
Not reaping any rewards
We just repeat the patterns
That determine who we are

So what is noble in emotions?
It is what leaves us vulnerable
To the very worst of being human
I have neither hope nor answers

*

524.

Discarnate souls
Disturbed by emotions
They cannot control

Unconscious patterns
Recurring devotions
To coveted matters

Lack of discipline
Mental illness
Total stimulation

Delusions we swallow
Can lead to downfall
Or keep us from feeling the pain
We cannot control
What others may choose
But holding on leads to more of the same

Try something different
Try something new
But change whatever it is that you do
That leads to the unpleasant
That clings to you

Like moss to a stone
It only grows thicker
Unless you move on
And change the picture
Within is the dawn
Outer darkness is quicker

Child of the Universe

Emotions cling to us
We dress ourselves in our pain
The burdens we carry
Are what is remembered
Inside the mind where we dream

Choose to stand alone
We seek comfort from others
When inwardly lies home
The direction is independence
As we become one
In stillness we find love

Choose to let go
Of pain that haunts
Choose to let go
Of what others want
Contemplate what you truly want most
Recognize the past that keeps you from it
And choose to let go

*

525.

A seed germinates instinctively
Grows automatically toward the sun
Life plan programmed genetically
But anything can happen

One has faith but does not know
How long the life?
How far to go?
How strong the strife?

What joy will flow?
Will one survive to complete the show?
Will life be shared or lived alone?

A beautiful flower can only grow
From deep within the dirt below

*

526.

People who act friendly
Are usually not friends
Those professing love
Are failures in the end

And people who need rules
Are afraid to bend
Those believing all they hear
Have nothing real to give

Child of the Universe

I can only concentrate
On just whatever is
And focus on what gives me joy—
The happiest way to live

No one sees the reasons
You choose who are your friends
They only see their actions
The flaws of which you sin

It's all behind your back
You don't know what's happened
But what some have done to them
Is blamed upon the friend

Or lover, spouse, or family
Just living in the open
While someone dark and dirty creeps
All reputations blacken

One can disassociate
While striving to forgive
But virtue does not reciprocate
Best to forget and live

The doctor says all writers
Suffer from depression
The cause is so much deeper—
The depth of one's perception

The writer strives for quality
The reader entertainment
Communication fails in spite
Of deepest introspection

*

527.

It's just business
What good is that?
That people live

But they must feel
For life is real
Through what we feel

*

528.

Groups are not for me
They always expect
What I cannot be
Following rules and formalities
Artificialities
What are they trying to be?
Keep up the walls
Maintain acquaintances
But no one's allowed
To develop friendships
Or depth
Ignore the rules
Go around the walls
People weren't meant
To have no soul

*

529.

Our founding fathers blew it
They were hypocrites
Wealthy landowners made a profit
From war that benefitted the rich

Child of the Universe

Sound familiar?
It continues
Shame on all
That live with it

Lincoln tried to fix it
Assassinated
And so we're stuck with divisions
Everyone makes a decision

How many wars have been fought
That benefit the rich?
How many more must die
Or live impoverished?

And so it goes
A flawed system
Devoid of kindness
That shames all living with it

How many politicians
Out to make a profit
Sentence many to die
Waving a flag lacking conscience?

All for a class system
Opposed by constitution
All for degradation
Of everything human

My country was founded by hypocrites
Promising false hope of idealism
My country only protects the rich
While destroying its own constitution

A fatal flaw
A rule of law
Not meant for all
Still time to right the wrongs

*

530.

Yes, I have delusions
Yes, I know the difference
They help me understand

Mental fabrications
Myths with symbolism
Older than the land

Dream interpretation
Mind communication
Has always been my friend

*

Child of the Universe

531.

Sleep releases us briefly
From the pain of everyday life
And reminds us this hell is not our true home
But the peace found deep inside

The currents on the surface are blown and battered
We dive for tranquility
And images with meaning that speak from under
The waves called reality

The world is weary
I am world-weary
The greed and hate seem too scary
I dive for safety and peace

May I not wake up one day
May I find the deep current and be carried away
If I must return may it be near the sea
May I remember at Castle Mey

*

532.

Comfort in seclusion
I embrace it
Returning to my old ways
Within my thoughts

My wall is my garden
My cloak of invisibility
Is natural beauty

*

533.

Moving into wordlessness
The world of music
Transitioning from songfulness
To vibrating strings
Peace in harmony
Vibration fulfilling
Stillness

*

Child of the Universe

534.

A place on earth
Free blowing wind
The ocean nearby
A warm fire within

To keep out the ice
Somewhere North
No need for noise
In a solitary village

Here I will live
Soft-spoken people
With whom to work
On something creative

This is how I wish
To live my next chapter
Quietly so I must be quiet
Peacefully so I must be peaceful

And I must learn to turn my back
When I smell the odor of adversity
I must learn to walk away
When others begin bickering

I've fought my last battle
No martyr lives here
I am what's left to conquer
I choose peace over fear

I am the novel
I must compose myself
For the lessons left to learn
Are locked within myself

*

Franki deMerle

535.

So many willing to follow new fads
That complicate explanations at a price
So many wanting to follow a path
Someone else tells them is right
So many wasting their money and time
To follow someone else
Each has their own path already laid out
They just have to trust themselves
How hard is that?
And it's free

*

536.

We say good-bye to meet again
We break and change and start again
A world full of souls afraid for survival
In a world taken over by the financially successful

No one wants to be on the bottom—trampled
Or lost and alone—forgotten
No one wants to be left out on the street
So some head for wilderness to seek retreat
And find nowhere left to run

We blame emotions for fear of feeling
But we are not hijacked by chemical dealings
Our hormones and nerves await our own choosing
To face them head on without fear or judging

*

537.

So much said is wasted breath
Drawn outward away from the center
Conscious breath
Vocal harmonies
Centered in absence of death

*

538.

Earth works through various densities
The plodding, well-grounded change ever slowly
Water is the essence of fluidity
No limit to calm or wave

Life comes from water
And feeds on the earth
A world full of matter
Illusions all outward

Air flows freest—mere subtle friction
No obstacles, no impediment
Waves of change and existence
Inner essence of life and probable prediction

But fire is thermal—spark of light
Defines the basis of connectivity
Directing air waves higher for flight
We escape the earth on waves of light

*

539. for the Dalai Lama

Such patience
Is inspiration
Much laughter
No consternation
Just kindness

*

540.

Gabriel, gentle Gabe
Lilies the colors of sunshine
The messenger tells the truth
When accepted sheds light on earth

Not the sun but the painter
Sharing portrayal of beauty
Simplicity often rejected
But offered

*

541.

Many have said I'm crazy
They don't see very deep
The surface air is hazy
We're all one underneath

*

542.

Snow at midnight
Soft and quiet
Blankets the earth with peace

Only the streetlight
Spotlights the moment
Silence requires release

A moment of respite
I am in it
Time and tension cease

*

543.

The window was broken
Glass shattered
It doesn't matter
Outside and inside come together

Displacement
Pushed aside
Replaced
Unable to hide

Never wanted to be there
Tried to do well
Not an obedient soldier
But my true self

Walls crumble
No matter how fortified
Illusions stumble
On reality and are mortified

*

Franki deMerle

544. for Justin

You touched me in a wondrous way
Nothing since have I perceived the same
"Meet me at the top of the world"
Past transgressions melted away

My silver dove
You sing and play
With love and grace

So many more have shared our dream
Because of the words you chose to sing
All silver stars sparkling
To be in such good company
In my wildest dreams

Kindness travels faster than light
Your voice is forever in my mind
And I answer
I am also here

*

545.

Humor
The evolution of a word
From when it was absent from facts
It wore a mask
A pretense of medical theory
Absent of feeling

Human
The evolution
The ability to laugh
At our own assumptions
Understanding of emotions
As more than hormones

Woman
Self-assertion
Happiness in independence
Freedom
To speak and laugh
And men listen

Religion
Ancient internal comprehension
Defies organization
Ritual dream reenactment
Not political or financial
But natural

Values
Life, love
Health of self and loved ones
Expression understood
Sharing Nature's truth
Open

*

546.

Chiana, the Panda Bandit Van-Alike of Vancouver
Angel hair soft and white
Fur that caresses in the night
Soft paw touch until the light

Mischief in those big green eyes
Huffs opinions much like sighs
Purrs and plays then runs and hides

Panda Bandit mask of black
Crescent moon shines on her back
Snow paws prance, the precious cat

Gymnast, Mighty Mouse, Panda Bandit
Cutie Cuddle, Charlie Chaplin, Ballerina
Snow Paws, Lady Love, my Chiana

*

547.

We find what beauty we love
We embrace it
We play with it
We make it our own
This is happiness
There's no power or control
We are one with it
It is us

*

548.

Roundness of river stones
Smooth to the touch
Sharpness can cut
But weathering heals

Revere the ancient
Where peace is within
Youth rushes about
Bustle and din

River stone comfort
To lie in peace
In any position
To simply be

*

549.

Spring frost upon white flowers
Cold sky bends and kisses earth
Warmth within melts the winter

Cleverness is admired
Beauty is overlooked
Truth permeates the world

Force yields triumphant
Anger bewilders
Serenity loves
Music overcomes
Words that silence stunned
Art has just been formed

A brief perception
It is a comment
Upon a moment

*

550.

Blossom on water
Floating but still
Creamy like butter
Beautiful, real

The peace of nothingness
Still frame of existence
Floating suspension
Quietly done
Perfection

*

551.

To the conscious
The unconscious is
Vast as the seas
The collective
Vast as the stars
Not me but we
One is
It's the zone
Of being free
Of letting go
And letting be

552.

Got off to a rough start in life
Really a fighter who barely survived
And cautious—
Can't be too careful
If you follow Gracie's rules
Everyone's OK

Genuinely gifted
Rascal mama's cat
Arias to Malagueña
Cattitude edged with sass
In vulnerability most precious
Extra stealth in her skill set

Gave us the time of our lives
Reaching to keep up with her
A bouncy, sassy gait
Cherished, cuddled and catered
In Gracie's eyes was understanding
Engineering in her brain

Graced our family
Removed fresh wall paper
Always busy
Caught on quickly
Investigated everything—
Electric plugs in play

Gentle being
Rest and come back
A lot I can learn still
Crafty clever cat
I'm grateful to know you
Exceptional silver cat

Child of the Universe

Goodness little Gracie
Rest peacefully sweetie
All the pain you hid is gone
Cat sisters miss you and will carry on
Into forever and into now
Everyone touched by you benefitted somehow

Gone too soon
Resplendent silk coat
And honey eyes
Cat extraordinaire
Intelligent beyond belief
Expressive personality

Gone to sleep peacefully
Ready we were not
A presence now missing
Cannot be forgotten
In the silence I wait to hear you say
Eck

Gone in a decade
Remains in our hearts
A lot of living so quickly
Caught us off guard
It was sudden but peaceful
Endings come to part

Gracie you are special
Remembering you will be easy
All for one—your trio
Chiana's oldest friend
I hope you will remember us fondly if
Ever you pass our way again

*

An Author's Note

I began writing poetry in my dreams when I was about 14 years old. Eventually I would wake up as I was writing, and finally I learned to write while conscious. For the first decade or two, I wrote in mirror writing. I have since broken that habit. *Ripples on the Surface* was my first collection of poetry. *Child of the Universe* is my second. I don't presume to know whence some of these thoughts arise, but I feel safe in saying they come from the unconscious.

I believe I began writing as a way of coping with troubling times and life conflicts. Now I write to express deep emotions, sort out what disturbs me, and express moments of peace and clarity, which fortunately come more frequently now. These are basic human expressions—expressions of living—of being. I've read that only one-tenth of a percent of human genetic material distinguishes us as individuals. It's our choice to see the forest or the trees. We, like all living creatures, are all children of the Universe, and like many, I am a child of the verse.

*

INDEX of First Line and Poem Number

A baby doesn't feel for others ... 507
A healer and a dancer ... 403
A leaf inspires ... 300
A long time ago ... 353
A pet is a master ... 346
A place on earth ... 534
A poet may be an idealist or cynic ... 464
A seed germinates instinctively ... 525
A world built of façade ... 358
Accelerate ... 463
An individual snowflake ... 481
Angels are the in between ... 352
Animals have no conditions ... 307
Arizona ... 158
Arte por Dios ... 158
As you read these lines ... 295
At most times it appears to me ... 492

Balanced like a razor's edge ... 419
Beaded with incense ... 293
Being nice is a tool ... 292
Blossom on water ... 550
Bongo ... 345
Buddy who came to visit me often ... 345

California ... 306
Can you ever just be you ... 449
Chiana ... 451
Chiana, the Panda Bandit Van-Alike of Vancouver ... 546
Chile ... 471
Clouds are swirling ... 290
Coast lined with sea lions ... 306
Comfort in seclusion ... 532

Communism died ... 393
Connecticut ... 347
Cousins live near Mystic Harbor ... 347
Child of the Universe ... 296
Country of value to the world ... 471
Cuddles for warmth and comfort ... 451

Darkness is a comfort ... 498
Dear John I am sorry ... 379
Definitions elude those without vocabulary ... 369
Delusion imagines states of perfection ... 422
Depression begins in repression ... 374
Depression is the poet's curse ... 317
Disappointment is an indication ... 424
Discarnate souls ... 524
Doubt is a curious thing ... 339

Each of us choose what we are part of ... 436
Earth works through various densities ... 538
Existence is ... 485
Every day we're given chances to be kind ... 465

Fate is carved like a coin ... 294
Few care about poetry anymore ... 320
First people fought for the right to life and liberty ... 515
For Adrian ... 518
For Aife and Barbara ... 432
For Arnetta ... 373
For BJ ... 479
For Bob ... 489
For Brother Cornel West ... 474
For Cam ... 392
For Carol ... 328
For Celia ... 395
For Christy ... 324

For Dawn ... 390
For Denise D... 312
For Dr. Bernstein ... 368
For Dr. Tom Dooley ... 516
For Steve Matous ... 470
For Elizabeth ... 382
For every day there is a season ... 308
For Gayle ... 400
For Jackie ... 336
For Joel ... 408
For John B ... 379
For Joy ... 356
For Justin ... 544
For Karen ... 370
For Kathy D ... 388
For Kathy L ... 522
For LVH ... 462
For Lewis Black ... 477
For Marla ... 403
For Marvin Bell ... 439
For Molly P ... 435
For Pete Bessas ... 365
For PTE ... 510
For Ray Young Bear ... 443
For Rhonda ... 332
For Richard Eberhart ... 499
For Richard Wilbur... 441
For Robin ... 397
For so long men have taught that women ... 406
For Terry ... 350
For the Dalai Lama ... 539
For Theodore ... 447
For Thomas Fallis ... 468
For Victoria ... 511
France ... 364
Freedom was born here ... 364

e

From a dream … 466

Gabriel … 410
Gabriel, gentle Gabe … 540
Generals of death … 341
Gentleness should owe no debt … 365
Gettysburg … 341
Got off to a rough start in life … 552
Gracie … 552
Greatness is only within the message … 410
Groups are not for me … 528
Groups that proclaim they are universal … 409

Happiness is natural … 330
Hawaii … 330
He said I didn't flirt … 437
Homeless camps behind grocery stores … 371
Hope you're well—I am … 470
How can one handle all of the pain … 296
How we work with words inside us … 500
Humor … 545

I cannot comprehend the chase … 313
I don't care for society's dictates … 512
I feel things deeply … 509
I find I get impatient with selfishness … 391
I find the gloom of minutia …416
I grew a purple flower … 298
I have a habit of seeking out men … 405
I have little energy left … 387
I have the luxury of illness … 361
I is for individual … 354
I like to think I'm progressing … 381
I live in a time when rappers … 378
I love glitter … 447
I love to be up in the trees … 441

f

I prefer the style of the cat ... 466
I spent a career serving a country ... 473
I worked with the French Resistance ... 407
I write for those who would understand ... 429
Ice, the crystalline beauty ... 377
Ici je suis ... 521
Idaho ... 313
Idealism does not contradict realism ... 417
Idealists do not survive in government ... 444
If the Chinese hadn't ousted him ... 299
Illness is a metaphor ... 337
Illumination of reflections ... 305
I'm better off a recluse ... 430
I'm not the saint that nurses the sick ... 376
I'm so grateful you survived the camps ... 518
In every church ... 459
Is one in need required ... 480
It isn't obsession with death ... 343
It's a choice ... 386
It's a nation of chemical dependence ... 442
It's difficult to shed the shackles ... 462
It's just business ... 527
It's OK to admit you're sad ... 310
It's real ... 315

Kansas ... 355
Kind assistance ... 468
Kindle what feels right ... 384
Kindling resentment of diversity ... 355
Kindness ... 384

La vida es buena ... 414
Lady Rainbow Goddess ... 367
Lasting logs ... 291
Letting go of what brings stress ... 475
Life is a work in progress ... 421

Life is hard … 349
Life is so hard for the wealthy … 430
Life itself has no titles … 434
Light comes down at all angles … 458
Little sister, the world can be cruel … 479
Look at the space in which you live … 398

Mais oui, mademoiselle … 338
Many have said I'm crazy … 541
Massachusetts … 309
May all beings … 412
May all people everywhere find … 412
May your cats only go in the box … 522
Memories are all we have … 396
Mercurial messenger hones her skill … 331
Mi guitarra canta … 359
Mined to death … 351
Miss you little lady bug … 456
Montana … 351
Moving into wordlessness … 533
Much time is wasted redefining … 415
Much time lived here … 309
Musette … 456
My body is aging and in pain … 505
My nightmares are returning to the past … 327

Nebraska … 325
Nestled in wet mountains … 334
Nevada … 316
New York … 360
Nice people wanting to lend a hand … 325
Nimble fingers reaching down … 360
No harm, no foul, no longer computes … 461
Nobody defragments cities … 344
None care about poetry anymore … 310
North Carolina … 334

Nothingness is something powerful ... 316
Now I see the fallacy ... 438

Of all the beings in the world ... 312
OK, I mix my pronouns up ... 460
Old growth shelters the new ... 297
One verse, one existence ... 311
Oregon ... 297
Others see who they want us to be ... 404
Our founding fathers blew it ... 529

Pain expresses displeasure ... 502
People do not fear the truth ... 427
People who act friendly ... 524
People with a scapegoat ... 497
Physical pain unrelated ... 411
Play your guitars my friends ... 472
Pour Soleil ... 338
Pourquoi dois-je faire des vers? ... 304
Pull out the scar tissue ... 506

Rayo viaja lejos de sol ... 103
Remembering is a blessing ... 402
Reset to default positions ... 389
Robin, sweet bird of song ... 397
Roundness of river stones ... 548
Rhythm is the heartbeat ... 496

Salty oceans swallow the snow ... 302
Seven wonders ... 291
Simple is enlightenment ... 380
Simplicity ... 495
Sleep releases us briefly ... 531
Small animals don't need our lifespan ... 455
Snow at midnight ... 542
So many archetypes ... 493

i

So many willing to follow new fads ... 535
So much a soul can understand ... 467
So much knowledge in the written word ... 363
So much said is wasted breath ... 537
Solitary thoughts ... 313
Some are born with prejudice ... 490
Some don't want to know what's wrong ... 413
Some look into a well ... 446
Some seek the placid water ... 423
Some women prefer women ... 452
Someone asked me once ... 425
Someone once coined the phrase ... 394
Sometimes the truth isn't pretty ... 335
South Carolina ... 357
Spring frost upon white flowers ... 549
Started the blood bath ... 357
Such patience ... 539
Sweetness of smell and taste ... 495

The airwaves are full of betrayal ... 469
The body breaks ... 486
The brain is imaginative ... 514
The Buddha ordained no clergy ... 385
The camera's eye sees the reality ... 392
The chains are broken ... 372
The crashes come more frequently now ... 383
The creator of this universe ... 329
The elemental play of change ... 318
The epiphany of justice ... 444
The flag of peace passed to the messenger ... 401
The flower sheds its seeds to the wind ... 489
The flutter of so many heartbeats ... 488
The knitting needles weave the blanket ... 342
The molecules form a body ... 523
The petals float on water ... 428
The petals open slowly ... 426

The scribe is but a messenger ... 483
The simple pleasure of going to sleep ... 348
The soldier is confident ... 504
The sunlight wrestles with the clouds ... 326
The truth is if you don't know the cause of the illness ... 399
The Universe bestows its gifts ... 520
The verses rise up from inside ... 491
The window was broken ... 543
The world is having a conversation ... 501
The world is imperfect ... 484
The young have no concept of consequence ... 478
There are milestones we pass unaware ... 321
There is no greater trust ... 370
There is so much negative ... 362
There's nothing like the fragrance ... 453
There's nothing progressive about life in the States ... 482
They say depression hurts ... 454
This world is such a violent place ... 519
To some I am an oddity ... 440
To the conscious ... 551
Trauma is invisible ... 516
Traumatized people fear change ... 333
Tunnel vision seems to be the default position ... 517

Vagrant leaves swirl around ... 319
Valley of lakes and Christmas trees ... 301
Vancouver, Washington ... 301
Vermont ... 319

We are the enemy ... 420
We as mortal beings ... 450
We come to Earth ... 476
We find what beauty we love ... 547

We have a global society ... 457
We have a purpose ... 314
We keep going as if we're getting somewhere ... 340
We live in a time of awakening ... 366
We live in the age of pushing buttons ... 418
We need food, water and shelter ... 482
We say good-bye to meet again ... 536
Welcome to our world ... 433
Western white isolation ... 322
What good is education not applied? ... 487
What is literal, what is metaphor ... 503
What percentage of the population is homeless? ... 448
What would Nature do for laughs ... 477
When does it stop ... 513
When you leave you don't take your things ... 508
Wisdom and education in combination ... 368
Woman on a power trip ... 510
Wyoming ... 322

Yes, I have delusions ... 530
Yes I would accept you ... 443
Yes there is eternity ... 439
You are a guardian angel ... 395
You are a traveler of the mind ... 388
You are my friend ... 332
You are the cobra rising up ... 350
You are the puzzle lady ... 382
You came to me at a crucial time ... 375
You have a laugh hearty and deep ... 328
You have so mistaken me ... 432
You have the key to peace ... 324
You have the patience of eternity ... 400
You have your life ahead of you ... 408
You know me well ... 435

You maintain perspective and speak the truth … 474
You met your mark … 499
You offered me friendship … 511
You paint what others do not see … 356
You restored my sanity … 373
You touched me in a wondrous way … 544
Young inquiring minds … 494
Your crown is the white of angel hair … 336
Your Goddess watches over you … 300
Your name is native to this land … 390

www.ingramcontent.com/pod-product-compliance
Lightning Source LLC
Chambersburg PA
CBHW070638050426
42451CB00008B/202